GW01087132

Jagdgeschwader 40(

Germany's Elite Rocket Fighters

OSPREY
PUBLISHING

Jagdgeschwader 400

Germany's Elite Rocket Fighters

Stephen Ransom and Hans-Hermann Cammann
Series editor Tony Holmes

Front Cover

On 11 September 1944, the Eighth Air Force mounted bombing raids on Ruhland, Böhlen, Brüx and Chemnitz, ten combat wings totalling 384 B-17 Flying Fortresses taking part in the attacks. The bombers were escorted by 275 P-51 Mustangs. The weather conditions over the target areas were cloudy. The attack began from an intercept point about 40km south of Merseburg at 1149 hrs. Ruhland, Brüx and Chemnitz were attacked at 1223 hrs from 24,500 feet up to 27,000 feet. Böhlen was attacked at about 1215 hrs. After the attacks the bombers reassembled at a point well west of the target areas at 1359 hrs.

Most of the ten bombers from the attack on Ruhland followed the planned flight path south of Brandis, the flight to this target being further south than the return route. The exception was a lone straggler heading for Ruhland from the 486th BG, 3rd Bombardment Division, which flew to the north – too close to the airfield at Brandis. Unteroffizier Kurt Schiebeler of 1./JG 400 was scrambled to attack. He later recalled;

'After my second sharp take-off, Oberleutnant Franz Rösle asked me, even though I had also made two sharp take-offs that day, to fly the third sortie for him. I took off in "White 2". There were bombers heading towards Dresden and a lone B-17 flew over the airfield. I flew towards the bomber too quickly and my shots went wide. I made a gliding second attack but again did not score any hits on the aircraft. During my third gliding attack, my shells hit the starboard inboard engine and it began to smoke. On my fourth gliding attack I raked the aircraft between the starboard engine and the fuselage. Two men bailed out and the main undercarriage dropped down. A voice from the command post called out "Turn back. The aircraft is beginning to go down". Hauptmann Robert Olejnik told me to fly a 90-degree course over the airfield and waggle my wings.'

The B-17 exploded on crashing near the village of Borsdorf about five kilometres west-northwest of Brandis. Three surviving members of the bomber's crew were picked up and brought to the airfield, where they met Schiebeler.

Dedication

To the former comrades of *Erprobungskommando* 16, *Jagdgeschwader* 400 and the IV. *Gruppe, Ergänzungsjagdgeschwader* 2, and the aircrews of the Allied air forces who met the Me 163 in combat.

First published in Great Britain in 2010 by Osprey Publishing,
Midland House, West Way, Botley, Oxford OX2 0PH, UK
44-20 23rd St, Suite 219, Long Island City, NY 11101, USA

E-mail; info@ospreypublishing.com

© 2010 Osprey Publishing Ltd.

A CIP catalogue record for this book is available from the British Library

ISBN: 978 1 84603 975 1
E-book ISBN: 978 1 84603 976 8

Series Editor Tony Holmes
Page design by Mark Holt
Cover Artwork by Mark Postlethwaite
Aircraft Profiles by Jim Laurier
Index by Alan Thatcher
Originated by PDQ Digital Media Solutions, Suffolk, UK
Printed in China through Bookbuilders

10 11 12 13 14   10 9 8 7 6 5 4 3 2 1

Osprey Publishing is supporting the Woodland Trust, the UK's leading woodland conservation charity by funding the dedication of trees.

www.ospreypublishing.com

The latter had been airborne between 1236 and 1250 hrs. The Me 163B that Schiebeler had flown in the attack, which was armed with MG 151 machine guns, was possibly one of the aircraft originally delivered by Hanns Klemm Flugzeugbau GmbH from Böblingen to Wittmundhafen and transferred with 1./JG 400 to Brandis in July 1944 (*Cover artwork by Mark Postlethwaite*)

CONTENTS

Me 163 EVOLUTION

Technologically, the Me 163 helped to develop high-speed, swept-winged, tailless aircraft aerodynamics and the use of liquid-fuelled rockets for aircraft propulsion. Paradoxically, testing of the Me 163 took place at a time when the high-speed characteristics of swept wings were still being measured and investigated in the wind tunnel. In October 1941, the aircraft was flown at more than 1,000km/h, setting an unofficial world record at a speed which the Me 262 did not achieve until 1944! The operation of the Me 163 also required the almost simultaneous development of handling and storage techniques for the highly volatile rocket fuel, special protective clothing for the pilots, high-altitude training for the pilots and radio navigation homing and interception methods.

The Me 163 rocket-powered interceptor was a natural progression in the development of aircraft in which Alexander Lippisch played a major role as designer and aerodynamicist. According to someone who worked with him and knew him well, 'Lippisch was a very determined man. He had his ideas and he didn't take no for an answer on anything that he tried to do. He had a very good relationship with his team. However, it was not always easy to work with him. He was also an artistic fellow – he had an interest in music, in painting and so on. He was very enthusiastic about things. With his team, it was always a matter of trust, and trust is a "two-way street". It was not always easy to convince him that a certain change was good for the overall benefit of a project or piece of work. But we all had a very, very good relationship with him'.

A further insight into his character can be gleaned from his own words at the time, when he was asked to consider a design for a rocket-powered aircraft. Lippisch later recalled the event in 1937 that was to prove a turning point in his career;

'At this time, we [the *Deutsche Forschungsanstalt für Segelflug* (DFS)] came under the RLM [*Reichsluftfahrtministerium*] *Forschungsabteilung*, with Dr. Adolf Baeumker as head of the department LC 1 and Dr. Hermann Lorenz as his assistant in charge of organisation. Dr. Lorenz and I did not get on very well. I was always doing something that was not on the agenda. Actually, it was not my fault. I was used to applying newly-acquired knowledge immediately in order to get ahead quickly and, of course, this did not fit into the well-ordered scheme of things in the research department.'

In the autumn of 1937, Dr. Lorenz came to Darmstadt to make an inspection of the work being done at the DFS on the propeller-driven DFS 194. He was also shown the DFS 39 (Delta IVc). During the course of the inspection Lorenz asked Lippisch which was the better of the two aircraft. Lippisch, on replying that he would choose the DFS 39, was then asked if he could build a second aircraft based on the DFS 39, but having a different fuselage to accommodate a new engine in the rear fuselage and a single-seat cockpit. Lippisch, apparently, guessed that the new engine would be a rocket motor, his surmise being

Alexander Lippisch in a contemplative mood. His interest in aeronautics was inspired by Orville Wright's flights at Tempelhof, Berlin, in September 1909. He lived a somewhat Bohemian and enterprising existence after World War 1, in which he served as an aerial reconnaissance photographic interpreter and cartographer on the Eastern Front. Lippisch's work at the Wasserkuppe from 1921 onwards led him to become a protagonist of tailless aircraft. In 1925, he was appointed head of the Technical Department of *Rhön-Rossitten-Gesellschaft* (RRG) Research Institute, at the Wasserkuppe, and produced the Storch and Delta series of gliders, motor-gliders and light aircraft. Before committing himself to a particular design he would often conduct tests with various relatively large scale model aircraft. In 1933, the RRG's Research Institute was amalgamated with the *Deutsches Forschungsinstitut für Segelflug* (DFS) at Darmstadt, where Lippisch continued to develop the Delta and other designs, including the DFS 194, forerunner of the Me 163. He joined Messerschmitt AG on 2 January 1939 to develop the Me 163, becoming head of Department L, but left the company on 28 April 1943 to take up an appointment as head of the *Luftfahrtforschungsanstalt* in Vienna. Lippisch was, however, retained as a consultant to Messerschmitt for further development of the Me 163 (*Fritz Stammer*)

later confirmed by Lorenz in the privacy of his office. It was planned to award a contract for a research aircraft for testing 'jet' propulsion at high speeds. Lippisch was to design an aerodynamically improved DFS 39 for the RLM's research department. This design was designated Project X with the security classification 'Top Secret', and it was the start of work on an aircraft which was to become the Me 163. Lippisch went to Berlin shortly afterwards to be initiated further into the mysteries of the project.

The contract called for the DFS to determine the aerodynamics of the aircraft and to build the wing in its workshop. The fuselage and engine were to be built in a special department under Heinkel but the DFS was to provide the drawings for the fuselage. For security reasons a special drawing office was fitted out at the DFS. This was furnished like a bank safe with the same sort of doors, which could only be opened if one knew the combination. Besides Lippisch, Josef Hubert and Fritz Krämer were also sworn to secrecy.

The Delta IVc received the type number DFS 39 and the serial D-ENFL. Heinrich 'Heini' Dittmar, who had joined the DFS in 1936, flew the Delta IVc at Griesheim for the first time on 9 January 1937. The aircraft enjoyed a relatively long life (Dittmar himself making 230 flights with it up to 24 August 1941) and was used not only for test purposes but also for ferrying passengers. Dittmar flew the Delta IVc to Augsburg on 19 April 1939 when he joined Lippisch at Messerschmitt as a test pilot. The experience with this aircraft undoubtedly influenced the design of the piston-engined DFS 194 (*JG 400 Archive*)

Ample funds for the project were made available. Wind tunnel testing of Project X was done at Göttingen from May to July 1938. The model retained drooped wing tips of the DFS 39 but had an aerodynamically clean fuselage. Tests with a large model of the DFS 194 powered by a petrol engine were done at Darmstadt to determine whether the lateral stability of the aircraft was acceptable. With a little persuasion, the Argus engine was started and the model flew across the airfield in a wildly unsteady manner. The model exhibited yaw/roll coupling oscillations caused by inadequate lateral stability. This characteristic was cured by fitting a fin to the rear fuselage, after which the model flew dead straight and disappeared from view in the direction of the Rhein-Niederung. The police located it later, some distance away. The wind tunnel tests in Göttingen showed similar, inadequate yawing and rolling stability. The

A model of the predecessor to the rocket-propelled DFS 194 with a piston engine was extensively tested in the wind tunnel at Göttingen between May 1937 and July 1938. This model had a planform similar to the DFS 39, with its propeller being driven by an electric motor. Both two-bladed and three-bladed propellers were tested (DLR Göttingen)

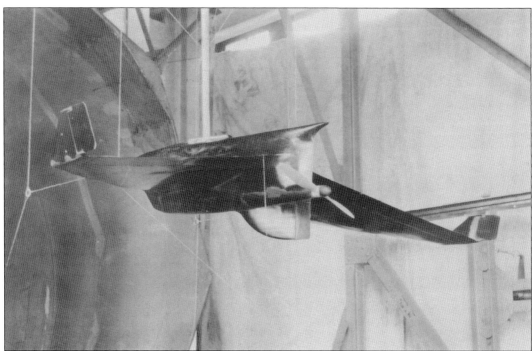

drooped wing tips were, therefore, removed and the wing rearranged to have no dihedral, and a fin was added to the fuselage. The results proved very satisfactory.

The design work, which was done in the secure office, progressed very slowly. The division of labour with Heinkel's department had also been organised in a complicated manner, and it was recognised that this arrangement would not produce positive results. In addition, Heinkel's main interest was the He 176 designed by Walter Günter, and so no real progress was made on Project X.

In the meantime, Prof. Walter Georgii and Fritz Stamer (Lippisch's brother-in-law) had drawn up a plan to move the DFS from Darmstadt to Braunschweig. When Lippisch was finally made aware of this plan, he was astonished to discover that the department for tailless research was to

Project X, two variants of which were tested in the AVA wind tunnel in May-July 1938 – one with drooped wing tips and no fin, which resembled the DFS 39, and the other without the drooped tips and with a fin (*DLR Göttingen*)

be disbanded and his staff transferred to other departments. Apparently, he was told that there was no immediate interest in tailless research as this sort of design was out of the question for military purposes.

As Lippisch's job at the DFS did not seem to offer much promise for the future, he decided to take up a position in the aircraft industry along with the best of his staff. Negotiations then started with Heinkel and later with Messerschmitt, which ended with Lippisch and 13 of his group from the DFS joining Messerschmitt AG in Augsburg-Haunstetten on 2 January 1939, where they worked in the newly created Department L (Lippisch). The group found themselves in a privileged position, as the project was classified 'top secret' and only Messerschmitt, his assistant, Joachim Schmedemann and Department L knew exactly what they were designing.

The new type received the designation 163A, the number being used to mislead those providing drawings for the components to be built in the experimental workshop. Schmedemann had suggested using the same number as that of a type already in existence, the Bf 163, which was a low-speed aircraft and a competitor to the Fieseler Storch. Three prototypes of this aircraft had been planned, of which only one is believed to have been built, but it did not fulfil the desired requirements, and the drawings designated 163A were, therefore, supposed to be of an improved version of this aircraft. Consequently, the first prototype received the designation Me 163A V4 (*Versuchsträger* 4).

The work on the 163A proceeded slowly. As it had been decided to increase the engine's thrust from 400kg to 750kg at full power, the original design had to be discarded and work on a new layout begun. Everything except the engine was to be built by Messerschmitt, the fuselage and centre-section of aluminium and the wings of wood. The

One of the two prototypes of the rocket-powered DFS 194, which was assembled at Augsburg before delivery to the *Erprobungsstelle der Luftwaffe* at Peenemünde. The fate of the other prototype is not known. Dittmar made the first towed gliding flight with the aircraft on 28 July 1939 and two further flights on the same day, the final of which lasted nine minutes. Dittmar flew the aircraft again on 4 and 5 August. These were the only entries concerning the DFS 194 made in his logbook. Dittmar did not record any of the flights he made at Peenemünde with the DFS 194 or the Me 163 (*JG 400 Archive*)

rocket engine was to be provided by Hellmuth Walter, whose company was located in Kiel.

When Lippisch left the DFS, Prof. Walter Georgii agreed to let Messerschmitt have the DFS 39 and DFS 194, which at that time was not quite finished. Lippisch's main concern was that there was nothing known about the rocket engine's performance and how it would influence the aircraft's flying characteristics. In order to gain some experience with this engine, it was proposed, therefore, to install it in a specially modified airframe of the DFS 194 and then test the aircraft in Peenemünde. As the airframe was not designed to fly at high speeds, the rocket engine's thrust of 400kg was considered more than enough.

At the outbreak of war on 1 September 1939, Department L's work was slowed down even more as the Me 163A was considered to have a low priority in the war effort. The modification of the DFS 194 airframe also began very slowly with so few people in the workshop. In the autumn of 1939 the DFS 194 was transported to Peenemünde, where it remained for just over a year, the last flight tests being conducted on 30 November 1940. All flight testing was undertaken by Heini Dittmar.

In 1940 the Me 163A reached an advanced stage of design and construction. The first towed flight of Me 163A V4 was made by Dittmar at Augsburg on 13 February 1941, delays in the delivery of the engine from its manufacturer, Hellmuth Walter KG, in Kiel, causing the first powered flight to be postponed until the following August. Although Generaloberst Ernst Udet had cancelled further flight testing of the He 176 shortly after the outbreak of war, he did sanction flight testing of the DFS 194.

The DFS 194 takes off from Peenemünde, where various tests with the aircraft were conducted between 16 October 1939 and 30 November 1940 (*EN Archive*)

Heinrich 'Heini' Dittmar successfully participated in various German model aircraft competitions held between 1925 and 1929 before joining the *Rhön-Rossitten-Gesellschaft* at the Wasserkuppe. While there he gained the A and B gliding licences. He went on to win various gliding competitions and establish world altitude and distance records. In 1937 he became the world champion at the first international gliding championship held at the Wasserkuppe, and was awarded the Hindenburg Trophy for Gliding Flight. In 1936 Dittmar became a test pilot with *Deutsches Forschungsinstitut für Segelflug* and, in 1939, joined Department L as a test pilot for Messerschmitt AG, Augsburg. He conducted the first flights of the DFS 194 and Me 163A. During flight testing of Me 163A V4 in 1941, Dittmar became the first pilot to exceed a speed of 1,000km/h, for which he was promoted to the rank of Flugkapitän and awarded the Lilienthal Prize for Aviation Research. In 1942 he was badly injured during flight testing of Me 163A V12. Dittmar resumed flying duties in 1944 (*EN Archive*)

In the summer of 1941, Department L's flight test group moved into quarters at Peenemünde and the people from Walter installed the engine in Me 163A V4. Heini was familiar with the aircraft's characteristics because of the gliding tests he had already carried out and, therefore, the initial flights got off to a good start. After take-off, the aircraft stayed close to the ground while gaining speed and then climbed steeply to an altitude of 4,000-6,000 metres (4,000 metres in 55 seconds from take-off). The flying characteristics were excellent. The success in 1941 was crowned by Heini flying faster than 1,000km/h.

At just over 1,000km/h the shock wave caused the airflow over the outer wing to separate suddenly and the aircraft pitched nose down, the instruments registering a negative acceleration of 11g. Heini pulled the throttle back quickly, the aircraft slowed down and he was able to take control again. In the evening the Askania theodolite measurements were evaluated, the final result revealing a speed of 1,003km/h!

Leutnant Rudolf 'Rudi' Opitz, who was to test the aircraft on behalf of the *Erprobungsstelle der Luftwaffe* at Peenemünde, later recalled;

'The speed record was actually set on the fourth flight of the research aircraft. When Dittmar made the first flight at Peenemünde, people from the High Command, Udet and elsewhere, were present. Of course, they were very impressed at what they saw and the climb rate of the aircraft. After this flight, Udet stopped the programme and ordered that no more flights would be performed until a second pilot was placed in the programme, since Dittmar was the only pilot at Messerschmitt who had flown the tailless aircraft. Udet realised that if something happened to Dittmar, all his experience would be lost.

'Messerschmitt were asked to recommend a pilot, and they wanted me because I had flown with Dittmar since the mid-1930s on flying wing research aircraft. So I got a call, and within a few days I was

transferred to Peenemünde. When I got there, Dittmar continued and made a second flight, which I observed. Then a day later he turned things over to me to make a short flight and I flew the aircraft. Then, on the fourth flight, they wanted me to follow a measured course over the Baltic to see how fast it could fly because up to that point only climbing flights had been undertaken.'

Me 163A V4 KE+SW at Peenemünde as it appeared soon after its arrival at the base in July 1941. This date conflicts with the information given on production and delivery schedules drawn up by Messerschmitt's planning department, which state that AV4 was delivered to Peenemünde on 17 April 1941. The entries in Dittmar's logbook show that he flew the aircraft at Augsburg up to 2 July 1941. After that date there is no mention of AV4 in Dittmar's logbook. Note the aircraft's high-gloss finish (*EN Archive*)

The Me 163A V4 flown by Dittmar was towed on its initial flights behind a Bf 110 piloted by Rudolf 'Rudi' Opitz, then still a member of the *Erprobungsstelle* at Peenemünde. At the beginning of August 1941 the aircraft had still not been fitted with a rocket motor (*EN Archive*)

Meanwhile, plans were being made for the production of the Me 163B, the armed operational variant, of which 70 were to be ordered.

The development of the Me 163B started on 1 September 1941, and a proposal containing a description of the aircraft and a schedule for its manufacture was submitted to the RLM for approval later that month. Production was planned to start on 1 October with the manufacture and assembly of four prototypes (V1 to V4) and an additional airframe for structural testing at Augsburg. The components of the remaining 66 production aircraft were to be produced at Regensburg and assembled at Obertraubling. The schedule was subsequently revised. That favoured by the RLM required the flight of the first production aircraft to take place seven months after the start of manufacture. Messerschmitt considered this to be unrealistic. The company thought that all of the aircraft should be regarded as pre-production machines, and it believed that the fifth example could not be delivered in less than 17 months.

Preparations for production did not actually start until December 1941 owing to the late arrival of the draughtsmen organised by the RLM. There were also delays resulting from the late delivery of the wind tunnel model and a lack of aerodynamicists. The shortage of materials was a more serious problem because it delayed the start of the manufacture of the production aircraft until March 1942, and the lack of information regarding the HWK and BMW engines and their installation also proved problematic. This particular issue was aggravated because these engines required different tank installations, as well as other airframe modifications that had to be made so as to keep pace with the engines' development. In addition, the engine proposed for the Me 163B, designated HWK RII 209, was cancelled and replaced by the RII 211. The aircraft then had to be modified again because the RII 209 and RII 211 required different propellant tanks.

The decision to fit the RII 211 created further delays, but it soon became apparent that Me 163B V1 would still be ready for flight testing before this engine could be delivered. Me 163B V1 was, therefore, designed to be equipped with the HWK RII 203 'cold' engine, which had been installed in the Me 163A but, in the event, BV1 was never flown under power.

The so-called 'cold' engine, designated HWK RII 203 by Walter and 109-509A by the RLM, was fitted to all Me 163As, except AV12 and AV13, and to BV4, BV6 and BV8. It was fuelled with *T-Stoff* (aqueous solution of concentrated hydrogen peroxide) and *Z-Stoff* (concentrated solution of sodium or calcium permanganate used as a catalyst). The Walter HWK RII 211 (RLM 109-509B) 'hot' engine was installed in the remaining Me 163B prototypes, except BV10 to BV14, which were reserved for BMW engines. The RII 211 was fuelled with *C-Stoff* (a mixture of hydrazine hydrate, methanol and water) and *T-Stoff*.

By May 1942 the production schedule had again been revised. Augsburg was now to be responsible for the manufacture and assembly of BV1 and BV6, of which the latter was to be fitted with a pressurised cockpit and an improved Walter engine, the 109-509 B-1. This rocket motor was fitted with an auxiliary combustion chamber known as the *Marschofen* to improve the aircraft's duration at cruising speeds. The

Paul Rudolf 'Rudi' Opitz was trained and employed as a joiner and cabinet maker, specialising in wooden aircraft construction. From 1935 to the outbreak of World War 2, he was a gliding instructor with the *Rhön-Rossitten-Gesellschaft* and the *Reichs-Schlepp- und Kunstflugschule* in Griesheim, and instructor and test pilot with the *Deutsches Forschungsinstitut für Segelflug* in Darmstadt. In September 1939, Opitz enlisted as a Flieger in the Luftwaffe, serving with *Sturmabteilung Koch*, with whom he participated in the attack with DFS 230 assault gliders on Fort Eben Emael and bridges over the Albert Canal, on the Dutch-Belgian border, on 10 May 1940. For his part in this attack he was awarded the EK I and promoted to Feldwebel. Thereafter, Opitz was assigned to the Gliding School at Hildesheim to help train pilots for this form of warfare, eventually taking charge of all airfields under the *Fliegerschule für Lastensegler* 4. As a Leutnant, he joined Department L, Messerschmitt AG, in August 1941, and was subsequently posted as a test pilot to Peenemünde to support the work being done by Dittmar. In May 1942, he joined EKdo 16 at Peenemünde and transferred with that unit to Bad Zwischenahn. Two years later, 'Rudi' replaced Hauptmann Otto Böhner as *Staffelkapitän* of 1./JG 400 after Böhner's accident at Wittmundhafen, and transferred with that squadron to Brandis. In October he was appointed acting *Gruppenkommandeur* of I./JG 400 in Wolfgang Späte's absence through illness, and on Späte's return to active duty was promoted to *Gruppenkommandeur* of II./JG 400 in November 1944, transferring with the latter unit from Brandis to Stargard and finally to Husum (*JG 400 Archive*)

remaining aircraft and the structural test airframe were to be completed by Messerschmitt GmbH at Regensburg. Production schedules were adjusted again in the late spring of 1943 when Messerschmitt was faced with further delays arising from slow progress with flight testing and a shortage of manpower to cope with the increasing demands placed on the company to develop and produce both the Me 163 and Me 262.

The situation was relieved to some extent by the RLM's demand that free capacity at Klemm's Böblingen factory should be used to produce the Me 163, and that Klemm should provide personnel to assist with final assembly of the Messerschmitt-produced aircraft. A formal agreement between the two companies resulted in Klemm undertaking final assembly at Lechfeld of all Me 163Bs starting with BV23.

Klemm was required to produce 30 aircraft per month, but initially there were a number of delays caused by alterations to the airframe, in particular by the installation of MK 108 cannon, which were fitted to all aircraft from BV45 onwards. Other modifications included the installation of additional armour plating around the cockpit, radio direction finding equipment, a buffer tank to guarantee fuel supply while the aircraft was accelerating, a tailwheel locking system, a dolly emergency jettison system, a thicker nose cone to compensate for additional engine weight, strengthened landing flaps, a revised tailwheel design and lifting points for ground equipment.

Initially, the prototypes were delivered to Bad Zwischenahn for acceptance flight testing by *Erprobungskommando* (EKdo) 16 pilots. In April and May 1944, acceptance tests were conducted by Karl Voy, Klemm's chief test pilot, at Wittmundhafen prior to the aircraft being handed over directly to 1./JG 400. In June, final assembly and testing was transferred to Jesau and in August moved to Oranienburg. After that date and up to the end of the year Klemm continued to deliver airframes to Junkers, who formally took over responsibility for the production of the Me 163 on 1 September 1944.

The production of components for the Me 163Bs delivered by Junkers was widely dispersed, final assembly taking place at Brandenburg-Briest and final inspection and acceptance flight testing at Oranienburg. Junkers allotted code names to the factories supplying the components to add further and deliberate confusion, the company designating individual or groups of factories after the names of places remote from the actual site of the factory. For instance, *Baugesellschaft Antonienhof* was centred on Brandenburg-Briest and *Baugesellschaft Wilheminenhof* on Oranienburg.

The first towed flight of BV1 KE+SX, was made by Heini Dittmar at Augsburg on 26 June 1942 – about one month later than had been planned the previous October. Although it was originally intended to fit the aircraft with a Walter rocket motor, KE+SX was never actually equipped with an engine. The aircraft was used for brake parachute, tailwheel and landing flap trials before being handed over, at the end of 1943, to EKdo 16 at Bad Zwischenahn, where it was used for pilot training. In July 1944, KE+SX was transferred to Brandis with *Ergänzungsstaffel*/JG 400, and later, also with that unit, to Udetfeld. (BV1 ultimately survived the war, and was among the Me 163s transported to the USA.)

Wolfgang Späte, who led EKdo 16 from April 1942 to May 1944, was promoted from Oberleutnant to Hauptmann at the beginning of September 1942. He was awarded the *Ritterkreuz* after 40 victories and Oak Leaves after 79 victories while serving with JG 54 in Russia (*JG 400 Archive*)

EKdo 16 was established in April 1942 to test and develop the Me 163 under conditions which were intended to lead to the production of an effective combat aircraft. The trials encompassed not only the development of the aircraft itself – airframe, rocket motor, ancillary equipment and weapons – but also all ground facilities needed to maintain and prepare it for combat. The unit was also tasked with the conversion training of pilots and groundcrew, and developing ground control techniques for the interception of enemy aircraft.

On 20 April 1942, the *General der Jagdflieger* charged Oberleutnant Wolfgang Späte with the establishment and leadership of EKdo 16 to test the Me 163A and Me 163B on behalf of the *Generalluftzeugmeister*, and to obtain information from the manufacturer regarding this completely new aircraft. Hauptmann Anton 'Toni' Thaler succeeded Späte as commander of the unit after the latter was posted to IV./JG 54 in May 1944.

On 26 March 1943, Lippisch was informed by Friedrich Seiler, Messerschmitt's chairman, that Oberstleutnant Georg Pasewaldt – the head of the development department GL/C-E in the RLM's *Technisches Amt* – had issued an order on 20 March requiring Department L to be absorbed completely within Messerschmitt's organisation. With the loss of his department, Lippisch tendered his resignation, which was accepted. His acquiescence in the face of this development, and the apparent rapidity with which it was carried out, indicate that it had been planned. The memorandum recording this event states that Lippisch was to take up a professorship in Vienna on leaving the company, and he was to be retained as a consultant to Messerschmitt AG. His consultancy fee was fixed at 5,000 Reichsmarks per year for a period of five years. Lippisch's contract with Messerschmitt was terminated on 30 June and his contract as consultant took effect the following day. Lippisch left Messerschmitt AG on 28 April 1943.

By the end of July 1943, EKdo 16 was expecting to test the first of the Me 163B series production aircraft at Bad Zwischenahn. The use of Lechfeld for this purpose was then being considered, but it was not anticipated that the airfield would be ready for acceptance flight testing of the Me 163 until the following March. In his report submitted on 3 August, Späte expressed his doubts as to the suitability of Bad Zwischenahn;

'In view of the change in the current situation in regard to air superiority, EKdo 16 has doubts as to whether all Me 163-related activities should be concentrated in Zwischenahn, since it is almost certain that the airfield will be attacked and valuable aircraft will be lost. It is proposed that orders should be issued for the immediate preparation of Lechfeld for Me 163 operations. Lechfeld could be prepared in a matter of weeks, since only propellant storage tanks and garages for fuel bowsers need to be erected. Lechfeld rather than Peenemünde could also be used to expedite company test flying by virtue of its proximity to Augsburg.'

Prototype flight testing began at Lechfeld on 13 September. Six months later the airfield experienced the first of a number of attacks, which put Me 163 trials and Me 262 production in serious jeopardy.

EKdo 16 drew up plans to transfer all aircraft and equipment immediately to Bad Zwischenahn because it seemed inadvisable to continue to base Me 163 flight testing at Peenemünde after the concentrated night attack made on Peenemünde-East on 17/18 August 1943 by 597 aircraft (40 of which failed to return) from RAF Bomber Command. EKdo 16 transferred most of its aircraft (seven Me 163As and one Me 163B, three gliders and five towing and courier aircraft), its available ground equipment and its personnel to Anklam on 18 August. The very bad surface of the airfield and the lack of ground facilities needed for Me 163 operations at Anklam, however, resulted

Activity at Peenemünde in the summer of 1943, with Me 163A V6 (CD+IK), AV8 (CD+IM) and AV10 (CD+IO) being readied for flight (*JG 400 Archive*)

in the transfer of the unit by rail to *Fliegerhorst* Bad Zwischenahn on 27 August.

The unit found that the special facilities required at Bad Zwischenahn had not been completed and, for this reason (as well as the need to maintain secrecy due to the presence of foreign labour employed in building work), training could not start before October. Furthermore, the contracts for the required ground equipment had not been placed. It was, therefore, agreed with the head of the Luftwaffe's training organisation that gliding training of pilots who were to report to EKdo 16 on 15 September would then take place at the gliding school at Gelnhausen (35km east of Frankfurt am Main) under the leadership and participation of officers from EKdo 16.

Pilot training at Bad Zwischenahn began in September 1943, but flight testing was prevented until the building work on the airfield had been completed and the builders, among them Danes, had been relocated and so were unable to watch maintenance activities and preparations for take-off. Their withdrawal was expected to take place at the end of October.

Of the 21 pilots who had begun training, one was dismissed because he proved unsuitable and 'showed a lack of interest' and another was returned to his previous unit for health reasons, although he was a good pilot. Conversion training was completed within seven days, and was immediately followed by towed training flights with the Me 163. On average, three or four flights were made by pilots, accompanied by an instructor, in two-seat gliders. These quickly showed that the pilots had developed bad flying habits which needed to be eradicated. However, they quickly adapted to the Me 163.

On 29 September EKdo 16 was informed by Dr. Höpfner, RLM Supply Office, that *C-Stoff* could not be delivered because the propellant was not available, and that the unit would have to wait three to four weeks because no transport and storage facilities were available either. Späte responded by stating in his monthly report that no take-offs could be made in Zwischenahn with the 'hot' engines and, therefore, operational trials with the Me 163B would have to be suspended if the delivery of *C-Stoff* could not be ensured. With regard to this situation, he pointed out that the production of *C-Stoff* was insufficient for the time when the aircraft would have to be used in earnest. Messerschmitt had been informed by the electro-chemical works Höllriegelskruth that, to date, production of the propellant was just enough to satisfy the requirements for engine acceptance tests at Walter, Kiel.

Under the direction of the *Institut für Luftfahrtmedizin*, Munich, 18 pilots with frontline operational experience who had been undergoing gliding training since the end of September participated in altitude acclimatisation training on the Zugspitze. This training was expected to finish at the end of October.

In late November, EKdo 16 was able to report that the pilots who had completed their altitude acclimatisation training on the Zugspitze had received further instruction at Bad Zwischenahn, and that the pilots who had finished gliding training were now making take-offs with the Me 163A towed by a Bf 110. Despite the foggy autumn weather, which had restricted flying to seven days, 16 pilots completed conversion training.

That month EKdo 16 suffered its first loss. Oberfeldwebel Alois Wörndl was killed on 30 November while flying Me 163A V6 CD+IK. The aircraft was completely destroyed. Späte recorded, 'The incident bordered on what we call in flying jargon "a total disregard for flying regulations"'.

The following month saw the unit's second casualty. On 30 December Oberleutnant Joschi Pöhs lost his life in an accident involving Me 163A V8 CD+IM. The aircraft's engine cut out just after take-off. He had not gained enough height to bale out, and he did not attempt to do so. Instead, Pöhs turned the aircraft back towards the airfield, banking it steeply during the turn. In doing so he was confronted with the antenna of the radio ground station. Having insufficient control to avoid it, Pöhs clipped the tower and the wing tip dug into the ground, sending the aircraft cartwheeling. A violent explosion followed. It was subsequently discovered that the undercarriage dolly, after it had been jettisoned, had bounced back higher than was usually the case and had struck the underside of the aircraft, rupturing a *T-Stoff* fuel line. Tragically, the safety device that had been built into the aircraft to register a decrease in

A direct comparison between the Me 163A and B. This photograph was taken soon after the first of the Klemm-built aircraft was delivered to Bad Zwischenahn in January 1944. Klemm completed all prototypes after and including BV23 (*EN Archive*)

the flow of fuel functioned exactly as it should have done and promptly shut down the engine.

Operational pilot training was hampered throughout February 1944 by poor weather, and the presence of enemy aircraft during the good weather. The Me 163A made 86 flights and the Me 163B completed 82. Hauptmann Robert Olejnik, who was designated to lead the first operational squadron, made his first powered take-off in an Me 163B during the course of the month.

On 30 March Hauptmann Thaler noted that at the beginning of the month EKdo 16 had nine operational Me 163Bs, of which only one had been cleared for flight. During March one aircraft was badly damaged and was being repaired and five more were delivered. As agreed, the aircraft from Klemm were delivered before they had been flight tested. Deep snow in Lechfeld was still preventing flight operations.

Between 30 March and 10 May two pilots in addition to Major Späte, Hauptmann Olejnik and Oberleutnant Opitz made powered flights with the Me 163B, and 33 pilots had each made their first 'sharp' take-off in those aircraft with flight-cleared engines (11 of them in Wittmundhafen). Towed flight training was undertaken by 12 pilots, and they were expected to complete this by the end of May.

The first operational sortie was flown by Major Späte in BV41 PK+QL on 14 May. He had no trouble locating the enemy aircraft following the directions transmitted by the *Nachrichtenoffizier* (Signals Officer). While approaching the target, Späte did not pay enough attention to his speed. He first realised his speed was too high when compressibility effects became noticeable and negative acceleration (experienced while manoeuvring the aircraft) caused the engine to flame out. He had reached an operational altitude of 6,500 metres.

Members of EKdo 16 take a break from flying. They are, from left to right (crouching), Josef Mühlstroh, Joachim Bialucha, Heinz Schubert, Rolf Glogner, (lying down) Mano Ziegler, Hans Bott and Hartmut Ryll (*JG 400 Archive*)

Unteroffizier Manfred Eisenmann and Unteroffizier Rolf 'Bubi' Glogner, the youngest of the Me 163 pilots, enjoying time off at Bad Zwischenahn. Eisenmann lost his life in a flying accident while serving with 2./JG 400 at Brandis on 7 October 1944 (*JG 400 Archive*)

During a second combat sortie made on 14 May by Späte, again in BV41, he was unable to locate his target. The lack of success was due to the compass giving a false reading and a faulty barometric altimeter. He also had trouble with the engine starter, which delayed his take-off. By the time this had been achieved the target was already receding into the distance. Späte was recalled after the enemy aircraft was more than 60km from the *Fliegerhorst*.

On 19 May Oberfeldwebel Nelte made his first operational flight with BV40. No contact was made with the enemy because the pilot did not precisely follow the course given by the *Nachrichtenoffizier*. Nelte had not yet had sufficient experience flying the aircraft.

A fourth sortie was made on 22 May by Oberleutnant Opitz in BV33 GH+IL. No contact was made with the enemy because there was eight-tenths cloud cover at 1,500 to 2,500 metres. The target was detected flying at 2,000 metres, and it was probably hidden by the clouds. BV33 was flown back to Zwischenahn without the pilot being able to see the ground.

Oberleutnant Langer flew BV41 on 28 May. Again no contact with the target was made. On this occasion the target was detected too late and the Me 163 took off too late. The approach directed by the *Nachrichtenoffizier* was followed correctly, even though the start was late. Langer was ordered to break off the attack after the Me 163 had flown more than 50km from the *Fliegerhorst*.

Oberleutnant Opitz flew BV40 on 29 May, the flight being made without ground control because the equipment was not working. The enemy aircraft was detected at an altitude of 12,500 metres and at a range of about 30km, and as it was drawing rapidly away from the airfield. No contact was made with the enemy because Opitz was tactically in the wrong position for an attack – he was too far behind his target to be able to cut him off. The flight was broken off at an altitude of 12,500 metres and Opitz had no trouble returning to the airfield.

During a second sortie made the same day, Oberleutnant Opitz came to within two kilometres of the target although the attack again had to be broken off but this time because it was hazy and he was flying into the sun. British Air Intelligence Department AI2(g) in its report No 3027 'Reported Interception of PRU Spitfire by Me 163' wrote of this attempt by Opitz;

'On 29 May 1944, an enemy aircraft, believed to have been an Me 163, attempted to intercept a PRU Spitfire near Wilhelmshaven. The pilot of the Spitfire has been interviewed by a technical intelligence officer and an account of the incident, with AI2(g) comments, is given below.

'1. The Spitfire was on a photo-recce flight in clear weather (vapour trail height 30,000 feet). It had made two runs over Hamburg and two runs over Bremen so that the enemy had ample warning of its presence, and the conditions were favourable for visual interception.

'2. At 1315 hrs, the pilot (hereafter referred to as "X") approached Wilhelmshaven flying northwest at 37,000 feet and turned to make a run from east to west. As he turned West he saw a white trail being formed by an aircraft which he estimated was 7,000-8,000 feet below him, and distant approximately 2,000 yards (horizontally) to the southeast. This aircraft was then flying North, and as he watched, X saw the trail turn sharply West following his own course, and formed the opinion that the enemy pilot was attempting to intercept him.

'3. After the enemy aircraft had completed its turn, the trail was interrupted and did not begin again until the aircraft had covered a distance corresponding to approximately three times the length of the trail formed. This procedure was repeated at apparently regular intervals until four lengths of trail were visible. Meanwhile X, who had started to climb as soon as he first saw the trail, had reached an altitude of about 41,000 feet. He estimated that the enemy aircraft was then 3,000 feet below him, and approximately 1,000 yards (horizontally) to the south-southeast.

'4. Thus, while X climbed about 3,500 feet, the enemy aircraft had climbed approximately 8,000 feet and simultaneously reduced the horizontal distance by about 1,000 yards. X could then see the enemy aircraft, but not sufficiently distinctly for positive identification. He described it as being "nearly all wing". He also thinks that the wing had pronounced sweepback, but states that the angle at which he viewed the aircraft makes it impossible to state this with certainty.

'5. No further trails appeared, and X lost sight of the aircraft and did not see it again. Meanwhile, he had almost completed his photo run. He returned to base without further incident.

'6. X's memory is by no means clear on the question of time, but this is understandable and does not detract from the value of his report. When questioned, for example, he expressed the opinion that perhaps 30 seconds might have elapsed from the time that he first saw the trail until it finally ceased. When it was pointed out to him that during this interval he himself had climbed approximately 3,500 feet, which must have occupied about three minutes, he seemed genuinely surprised.

'7. He then thought that possibly there might have been more vapour trail patches. On the whole, it is felt that his visual impression of four patches, as first described, is more likely to be correct.

'8. On this basis of four cycles in about three minutes, it would appear that the power unit of the enemy aircraft was being cut in for 11 seconds, and then cut out for about 33 seconds. Admittedly, owing to variations in speed, the time ratio would not exactly conform to the distance ratio, but it would not differ appreciably from the estimated 3:1.'

Post-war research identified 'X' as Flt Lt G R Crakanthorp DFC, serving with No 542 Sqn RAF. This was Crakanthorp's 102nd operational mission, and he flew Spitfire PR XI MB791 on this occasion. The sortie was regarded as successful and the pilot returned safely to RAF Benson with 500 exposures. Crakanthorp's luck ran out on Monday, 27 November 1944, when he was shot down by Feldwebel Horst Lennartz of III./JG 7 flying a Me 262 near Stuttgart. He had made repeated runs over Munich on this, his 138th sortie, in Spitfire PR XI PL906, and was returning to England when bounced from behind and below. Crakanthorp baled out and was taken prisoner. He survived the war.

On 30 May Bad Zwischenahn was targeted by USAAF bombers, the attack taking place at 1040 hrs. The cleverly planned raid from three directions did not allow sufficient time to sound the alarm and to remove all aircraft from the airfield, but all important items of ground equipment and spare parts had already been stored elsewhere. EKdo 16 lost two men, who were manning a machine gun post on the airfield. According to the loss report issued by *Gen.Qu.6.Abt.(V)* on 10 June 1944, the following Me 163s were destroyed or damaged during the attack, along with 23 other aircraft. The extent of the damage to each aircraft is quoted in brackets following the *Werknummer* (Wk-Nr.). Total destruction is noted as 100%;

BV33 Wk-Nr. 16310042 (100%)
BV14 Wk-Nr. 16310023 (10%)
BV12 Wk-Nr. 10021 (30%)
BV21 Wk-Nr. 10030 (25%)
BV45 Wk-Nr. 10054 (15%)
BV47 Wk-Nr. 10056 (15%)

After the attack on Bad Zwischenahn, no work could be done on the remaining aircraft before 10 June (there was no water and electricity available and the damage was still being repaired). Basic training with the Me 163 was, therefore, transferred to Brieg on the Oder on 7 June according to an order issued by OKL *General der Flieger-Bodenorganisation* five days earlier. During two telephone conversations with *Luftflotte Reich*, the *Kommando* emphasised that training could only begin, however, once the tactical reconnaissance group based at Brieg had been relocated. It became evident that both units could not use the same airfield since, on the one hand, the reconnaissance group was flying 10,000 to 12,000 sorties each month with Ar 56s, Fw 56s, Bü 131s and Bf 109s and, on the other hand, the *Erprobungskommando* could only make towed starts in an east-west

Oberleutnant Franz Medicus gained his gliding licences at the schools at Wangen/Allgäu and at Hesselberg, near Gerolsfingen in Bavaria. At Hesselberg he was retained as a gliding instructor, eventually becoming the head of the gliding school. While there Medicus also gained powered aircraft licences. In 1940 he completed a flying instructor course at Brandenburg-Briest and afterwards taught at Kaufbeuren and Gelnhausen. Medicus served with JG 104 from October 1943 onwards, transferring to EKdo 16, then at Bad Zwischenahn, in February 1944. A few months later he was given command as *Staffelführer* of *Ergänzungsstaffel*/JG 400 at Brandis. From October 1944 to February 1945 Medicus served with 6./JG 400, and afterwards until the end of the war with 5./JG 400 (*JG 400 Archive*)

direction, during which normal flight operations would be endangered by the jettisoning of the undercarriage dollies.

The training school arrived at Brieg on 10 June and the disassembled aircraft and spare parts were stored in a small building used by transport vehicles, but it was not possible to re-assemble the aircraft because there were no hangars or workshops available. Despite repeated demands by EKdo 16 the situation remained unchanged and, consequently, no flights were made at Brieg.

Flying recommenced on 15 June at Bad Zwischenahn with two of the prototypes, and 11 powered and seven towed take-offs were made. During one of the towed starts on 19 June, the pilot, Oberfeldwebel Nelte flying BV38 GH+IQ, had to make an emergency landing from a height of 50 metres over Lake Zwischenahn after one of the engines of the towing aircraft had cut out. His speed was 220km/h and a tailwind of 40km/h was blowing. The aircraft touched the water and somersaulted after bouncing twice. The canopy broke up and the pilot was able to rescue himself by climbing onto the wing.

In July 1944 an *Ergänzungsstaffel* (auxiliary squadron) attached to JG 400 was formed under the leadership of Oberleutnant Franz Medicus. It comprised six aircraft: AV10 (CD+IO), AV11 (CD+IP), AV13 (CD+IR), BV1 (KE+SX), BV4 (VD+EN) and BV8 (VD+ER). Apart from AV10, none of the other aircraft was fitted with rocket engines and, therefore, there is no doubt that the unit also had its own towing aircraft, possibly a Fw 56 *Stösser* or a Fw 44 *Stieglitz*. The *Ergänzungsstaffel* was

solely employed in training pilots for JG 400's operational squadrons and was transferred to Brandis in July.

At about this time (certainly before 23 August 1944) EKdo 16's remaining Me 163s were completely repainted in a new camouflage scheme and the aircraft were given two-digit numbers prefixed by the code C1, denoting EKdo 16. The numbers were white and the code, in much smaller lettering, was painted in black. The new camouflage scheme eradicated the previous identities of the aircraft. Fortunately, sufficient contemporary documents have survived to allow at least some of the old and new identities to be matched as follows;

High-scoring ace Major Walter Nowotny visited EKdo 16 at Bad Zwischenahn during the summer of 1944. These pilots are, from left to right, Nowotny, Franz Rösle and Kurt Schiebeler. Nowotny was noted for his unconventional uniform! He was shot down and killed on 8 November 1944 (*JG 400 Archive*)

C1+01	GH+IG	BV28	Wk-Nr. 16310037
C1+02	GH+II	BV30	Wk-Nr. 16310039
C1+03	?	BV40	Wk-Nr. 16310049
C1+04	PK+QL	BV41	Wk-Nr. 16310050
C1+05	PK+QP	BV45	Wk-Nr. 16310054
C1+06	PK+QR	BV47	Wk-Nr. 16310056
C1+07	Not identified		
C1+08	Not identified		
C1+09	Not identified		
C1+10	Not identified		
C1+11	VD+EP	BV7	Wk-Nr. 16310016
C1+12	VD+EW	BV14	Wk-Nr. 16310023
C1+13	GH+IN	BV35	Wk-Nr. 16310014

C1+11 was reallocated to Klemm-built Me 163B-0 BQ+UK Wk-Nr. 40008 after the destruction of BV7 on 11 September 1944. This list probably also includes BV12, BV21 and BV39, and a fourth aircraft, which has not been identified. It is evident from the list that there is no sequential relationship between the old and new identities.

On 15 August 1944 Bad Zwischenahn was attacked by 120-140 bombers. Thereafter, the whole of EKdo 16 was employed filling in bomb craters on the airfield and runway No 2 from 16 to 23 August. Afterwards, surplus technical personnel were employed repairing other damage around the airfield. Flight operations were expected to resume around 4 September, but they in fact began on 23 August, take-offs being made from an almost 1,000 metre-long strip in an unfavourable wind direction. The day ended in tragedy when Feldwebel Reinhard Lukas was killed in the attempt to land his aircraft, Me 163 BV28 C1+01. The wreckage was later delivered to *Fliegertechnische Schule* II at Fassberg for instructional purposes.

Flying operations recommenced after a pause of 23 days following the bombing with the completion of repairs to runway No 2. The number of aircraft available to EKdo 16 had by then been reduced from 15 to six as a result of the bombing raids on 30 May and 15 August and through non-serviceability. Despite the difficulties in obtaining spare parts and in repairing damaged aircraft, 33 'sharp' starts were made during September.

In August 1944 EKdo 16's remaining Me 163s were repainted with a new camouflage scheme and the aircraft given two-digit numbers prefixed by the code C1. BV45 was given the call sign C1+05 (*EN Archive*)

Generalmajor Adolf Galland, *General der Jagdflieger*, visited EKdo 16 at the beginning of September and informed the *Kommandoführer*, Hauptmann Thaler, that the unit would be disbanded. Thaler pointed out that it would be ridiculous to disband the unit before the Me 163B had begun operations in earnest. Generalmajor Galland's proposal to reduce the size of EKdo 16 to 40 men and merge it with the *Ergänzungsstaffel* at Brandis was also considered unacceptable. Thaler believed that it was absolutely essential to conduct intensive flight testing and ground equipment trials with new aircraft, especially with the Me 163, and that it was impossible to conduct fruitful trials within a short period of time with only six aircraft to which modifications were continually being made, and for which it was difficult to obtain spare parts.

Thaler argued that both attacks on Bad Zwischenahn (on 30 May by about 80 bombers and on 15 August by between 120 and 140 bombers) showed that the enemy was determined to keep the number of Me 163s low. The very difficult task of evacuating everything to safe areas had paid off and the aircraft and special equipment were not damaged, particularly during the second attack.

The *Erprobungskommando* was, therefore, surprised to receive the order, issued on 21 September, to transfer to Brandis. The more so since Thaler knew that the airfield at Brandis was already overflowing with aircraft from an He 177 bomber group (II./KG 1), an He 177 *Ergänzungsgruppe* and Junkers' flight test department (*Abteilung* 700). It was also intended to concentrate all flight testing, weapons trials, training, both 1./ and 2./JG 400 and EKdo 16 at Brandis, which was already in danger of being bombed. Brandis' unfavourable position, unlike that of Bad Zwischenahn, would prevent the aircraft from being evacuated to safety in the event of an attack.

A normal attack by 150 bombers would completely destroy the development of the Me 163 along with training and operations within a few minutes, or set back these activities by up to six months. Thaler, on receiving the transfer order, spoke with Oberst Gordon Gollob personally in Berlin and explained his reservations about the move. Gollob supported Thaler's viewpoint and ordered him to delay carrying out the order. The above mentioned reasons for not complying with the order were sent by telex to the KdE Rechlin, Oberst Petersen. Thaler, however, was ordered once again by telex on 30 September to transfer immediately to Brandis. This order was carried out.

Thaler's fears concerning the bombing of Brandis did not materialise, for it was bombed only once, on 28 May 1944, although USAAF bombers turned over the airfield to attack targets close to Merseburg and Leipzig from the east, i.e. on the homeward run. The Allies were aware of the Me 163s at Brandis through the encryption of German radio traffic and the combat sorties flown by JG 400 against the Eighth Air Force's bombers from the end of July to the middle of September. If, as Thaler thought, the Allies were determined to reduce or eliminate the force of Me 163s, then they had ample opportunity to bomb Brandis, but they chose not to. The Allies were more determined to destroy the oil refineries at Merseburg-Leuna, Lützkendorf, Böhlen and Rositz.

1. *STAFFEL/ JAGDGESCHWADER* 400

In December 1943 the preparation of the various airfields planned for Me 163 operations was proceeding at quite different rates. The installations at the airfields within the responsibility of *Luftgau* Holland were then more complete than those in various parts of the homeland, the airfields at Venlo and Deelen being ready apart from the installation of *C-Stoff* storage tanks, which had not yet been delivered. The building work at Venlo and Deelen had taken just under six weeks. EKdo 16 was to complain that the same work at Bad Zwischenahn was unlikely to be completed in under seven months! EKdo 16 also noted in December that the airfields at Wittmundhafen and Oranienburg were almost complete as well, and those at Husum and Brandenburg-Briest, where there were already many suitable buildings that could be used, were expected to be ready in the near future.

It was anticipated that the airfield at Twente would be available at the end of March 1944 but there was still uncertainty as to whether the airfields at Achmer, Nordholz and Parchim would also be ready at that time, even though this had been promised by those in charge of the building work.

Orders for the formation of the first of the operational Me 163 squadrons were probably issued at the end of 1943, even though plans for its creation had long since been made. The existence of the squadron, then designated 20./JG 1, was first mentioned in the *Luftflotte Reich* order of battle dated 31 January 1944, and its presence at Wittmundhafen was registered between 21 February and 15 March. This squadron was renumbered 1./JG 400 sometime during February, and according to official documents was based at Wittmundhafen from 18 March until 24 July 1944. These dates do not correspond with those of events recalled and noted by members of the squadron.

At the time of its formation, 20./JG 1 shared the airfield with 2./NJG 3 and *Staffeln* from III./NJG 1 and II./KG 54. From March onwards, the airfield was used also by *Staffeln* from I./ and III./KG 54. At the beginning of June, 1./JG 400 appears to have been the sole occupant of the *Fliegerhorst*.

Groundcrews for the operational squadrons, and for EKdo 16 itself, began to arrive at Bad Zwischenahn between 4 and 8 January 1944. There they were given practical instruction in all aspects related to pilot training and trials with the Me 163 during the following four weeks.

The Y-ground station at Wittmundhafen had been continuously manned since 1 February 1944 and was being used to improve radio navigation methods. The ultra-short wave Adcock radio beacon installed there was also operational. The command post at Wittmundhafen, however, was not at that time fully equipped because it had been difficult to obtain the required communications equipment, and a temporary communications network had had to be established to overcome this difficulty.

Ground controllers for the *Würzburg-Riese* radar installed at Wittmundhafen arrived during February. It was discovered soon afterwards, however, that they had been given only two hours of instruction concerning the radar's operation, during which time the radar had not even been switched on! EKdo 16 also found out that almost all of these soldiers had only been employed on everyday tasks in their previous unit. This incredible situation provoked the *Erprobungskommando*'s signals officer, Leutnant Gustav Korff to make a formal complaint to the head of the Luftwaffe's *Nachrichten- und Verbindungswesen* (Signals and Communications Department), and EKdo 16 to comment in their monthly progress report;

'It is impossible to believe that these men can be entrusted to operate the *Würzburg-Riese-Gustav* equipment, and that they will be able to play a valuable part in the work to which they have been assigned.'

Subsequently, the soldiers were placed under the supervision of Unteroffizier Leisten and were given the task of preparing the *Würzburg-Riese* for operational use.

Hauptmann Robert Olejnik received his orders to prepare for the establishment of the first operational squadron during a visit to the *General der Jagdflieger* at Berlin-Gatow on 20 February 1944. The personnel, pilots and groundcrews to be transferred from EKdo 16 had already been selected. All of them were transferred to the new squadron, which was to be based at Deelen, with effect from 1 March 1944. After that date the squadron became a fully autonomous unit in accordance with orders issued by the *Oberkommando der Luftwaffe*. While preparations for the transfer to the new airfield were being made, Olejnik received a secret telex from the office of the *General der Jagdflieger* informing him that, because of its position, Deelen could no longer be used for Me 163 operations and that the unit would be based instead at Wittmundhafen. Everything then had to be rearranged as quickly as possible and the advance party had to be recalled from Deelen.

Soon afterwards, Olejnik received another telex from the office of the *General der Jagdflieger* confirming the establishment of the squadron with effect from 1 March 1944, and naming it 1./JG 400.

The move was accomplished with the help of Wittmundhafen's *Fliegerhorst-Kommandant*, Major Mewes, within a few days, and on 7 March the unit celebrated its formation with guests from the *Fliegerhorst* and Bad Zwischenahn. The youngest member of the squadron, Leutnant Bott, noted those present on a commemorative cartoon. They were;

Pilots – Hauptmann Robert Olejnik, Oberleutnant Gerhard Eberle and Franz Rösle, Leutnant Hans Bott, Oberfeldwebel 'Fritz' Husser and Siegfried Schubert, Feldwebel Hans Wiedemann and Friedrich Oeltjen and Unteroffiziere Kurt Schiebeler and Rudolf Zimmermann.

Ground personnel – *Nachrichtenoffizier* Oberleutnant Friedrich, *Technische Offiziere* Kern and Oberleutnant Ernst Siebert, Prüfmeister

Hauptmann Robert Ignatz Olejnik served with 2./JG 3 and 4./JG 1 from 1936 to May 1943, when he temporarily took over command of II./JG 1. In July 1943 he was promoted to *Gruppenkommandeur*, III./JG 1. He was awarded the EK II on 9 September, the EK I on 30 September 1940 and the *Ritterkreuz* as Oberleutnant on 30 July 1941 (41 victories). Olejnik joined EKdo 16 in October 1943 and was appointed *Staffelkapitän* of 1./JG 400 at Wittmundhafen in March 1944. He returned to duty at Brandis in mid-July after recovering from a take-off accident with Me 163B V16 at Wittmundhafen on 21 April, resuming command of 1./JG 400 in September 1944 (*JG 400 Archive*)

Leutnant Hans Bott, born 16 March 1921, began his basic training with powered aircraft in 1941 at *Flugzeugführerschule* (FFS) A/B 10 at Warnemünde and subsequently became an instructor with the same unit. He then trained with JG 106, Lachen-Speyerdorf, and JG 104, Fürth, to become a fighter pilot. He served with EKdo 16 (November 1943 – February 1944) and afterwards joined 1./JG 400 at Wittmundhafen. There he was the only pilot with no combat experience as a fighter pilot (*JG 400 Archive*)

Hauptmann Robert Olejnik, *Staffelkapitän* of 1./JG 400, and Oberleutnant Franz Rösle (*JG 400 Archive*)

Oskar Unterhuber, Oberfeldwebel Freiburg (*Spiess*), Oberwerkmeister Iser and Flieger-Hauptingenieur Brede.

The guests included Stabsartz Dr. Melchior, Oberleutnant Franz Medicus and Leutnant Hermann 'Mano' Ziegler.

Leutnant Hartmut Ryll, Feldwebel Herbert Straznicky and Unteroffiziere Anton Steidl and Schametz were to join the squadron at a later date. Fritz Husser was posted to the second *Staffel* in July 1944.

The first operational Me 163 was delivered by Oberleutnant Opitz to Wittmundhafen on 10 March 1944. All of the Me 163s that were to be transferred from Bad Zwischenahn to Wittmundhafen were towed there by a Bf 110 to avoid the necessity of disassembly and reassembly. Three of the first five operational aircraft were expected to be delivered by 10 April and the remaining two by 20 April. Delivery records for this period are incomplete but BV9, BV16, BV20, BV29 and BV34 were among the earliest aircraft transferred to Wittmundhafen. BV16 was delivered on 29 March.

Flying began on 15 March 1944. There was, however, a shortage of water needed to prepare the Me 163s for flight – for flushing the propellant tanks and diluting fuel which had spilled or leaked on to the ground. There was not even enough water in the *Fliegerhorst*'s storage tanks for this purpose. The squadron, therefore, had to resort to drilling its own wells, but even after boring down to 100 metres these still did not deliver sufficient water. After obtaining permission from the *Luftwaffenführungsstab* to drill deeper, an adequate water supply was found at a depth of 142 metres.

On 12 March 1944, the squadron received a telex from the *Luftwaffenführungsstab* via the *General der Jagdflieger* forbidding it to fly combat sorties, in order to avoid drawing itself to the attention of the Allies but permitting it to practise firing during daily exercises. Combat training with live ammunition had been neglected up to that time, but

Unteroffizier Kurt Schiebeler, Feldwebel Siegfried Schubert and Unteroffizier Hans Wiedemann, Wittmundhafen, spring 1944 (*JG 400 Archive*)

this situation was subsequently remedied by the pilots' making two or three 'sharp' starts per day with either full or half loads of ammunition.

Since both of the weapons which had been installed in the Me 163, the 20 mm calibre MG 151 machine guns and the 30 mm MK 108 cannon, had already been proven in combat, the exercises concentrated on firing the guns at high altitude or during high-speed turning manoeuvres. Holes in, or tips of, clouds were among the targets used by pilots.

No problems were experienced while firing in straight and level flight but as soon as attempts were made to fire at 800km/h or more during tight turns the ammunition belt links broke apart – the guns themselves had to drag the long ammunition belts from their tanks located in the fuselage to bring the rounds into position for firing. Olejnik proposed installing drum-fed ammunition to avoid the lengthy development of new belts which could sustain the forces exerted during these manoeuvres. Subsequent flight tests with this arrangement proved successful but the idea was not adopted.

Permission from the *Luftwaffenführungsstab* to begin combat operations was still not forthcoming even though it was noticeable that the Allies, after about the beginning of April, had increased their number of reconnaissance sorties. At least two or three high-flying aircraft, mainly Mosquitos, were observed crossing over the airfield daily, their vapour trails allowing them to be easily tracked. The squadron was ordered to bring its Me 163s under cover every time an enemy aircraft was spotted. The personnel were also ordered to take cover outside the airfield, in foxholes, in bunkers or in the nearby woods. This situation, naturally, led to disruption of flight operations and maintenance work, and demoralisation of the squadron's members.

On 21 April, the spate of engine problems, then being experienced soon after take-off at Bad Zwischenahn, was to claim yet another victim, this time at Wittmundhafen. Olejnik, who had already flown about 15 firing exercises and was thinking that this would be the last he would have to make, had donned his protective flying suit and was sitting in his aircraft, BV16, preparing to take-off when he received the radio-telephone message that enemy aircraft were approaching and his aircraft, with full tanks and loaded with ammunition, would have to be 'hidden'. Once the 'all clear!' had been given, about an hour and a half later, he again prepared to take-off.

Just after the aircraft had lifted free of the runway and the dolly had been jettisoned, the Me 163's engine began to lose thrust and the aircraft felt as though it was no longer flying trimmed. Then the thrust dropped off even more quickly, at which point Olejnik decided to shut down the engine completely and jettison the remaining fuel. After narrowly avoiding a Flak tower, he managed to make an emergency landing in a field. He landed with the skid retracted at about 340km/h and, as the grass was wet, slid about 600 metres before coming to rest.

While climbing out of the cockpit on to the wing, and from there to the ground, he noticed that the engine was on fire. He then realised his face was bleeding and that something was wrong with his back but he managed to drag himself a few metres away from the aircraft before collapsing. The aircraft exploded a few seconds later and soldiers from the Flak tower quickly appeared on the scene. They ran round the aircraft but became resigned to the fact that they could no longer be of help until they found Olejnik lying on the grass. Warding off attempts to help him, Olejnik decided to wait for the ambulance and the accompanying doctor, who, unfortunately, had only been with the squadron for two or three days and who had, therefore, had no experience with casualties from Me 163 accidents. Olejnik was taken to the naval hospital at Sanderbusch, where he was treated for head injuries and compressed vertebrae. He remained in hospital until the end of June, when he discharged himself, still encased in plaster, in order to resume his command.

Olejnik's position as *Staffelkapitän* of 1./JG 400 was filled, at the beginning of May, by Hauptmann Otto Böhner. Until the appointment of Böhner, Oberleutnant Eberle had been Olejnik's deputy and, through Eberle, Olejnik had been able to maintain regular contact with the squadron. The cause of the accident had, in the meantime, been traced to a leak in the *T-Stoff* fuel flow regulator, the fuel eating through one of the regulator's artificial rubber seals. Hauptmann Böhner himself was to be injured in a hard landing on 28 May.

The squadron began to receive more aircraft, mainly from Klemm's factory at Böblingen, towards the end of April and throughout May 1944. Karl Voy, Klemm's chief test pilot, was sent to Wittmundhafen to conduct acceptance flight testing of the aircraft before they were formally handed over to JG 400. Included among the aircraft delivered at that time were BV43, BV44, BV46, BV50, BV52, BV54-BV57 and BV59. Of these, BV43 was returned to Lechfeld for modifications on 14 June. This aircraft was almost totally destroyed at Lechfeld during the bombing raid carried out by the USAAF on 19 July and was not rebuilt. BV57 and BV59 were later transferred to Jesau and Oranienburg respectively for reasons still to be determined. Series production aircraft began to arrive at Wittmundhafen after the middle of May, the first of the batch, Me 163B-0, BQ+UD, Wk-Nr. 440001, being tested there by Karl Voy on 26 May. At the end of the month all acceptance flight testing of Klemm-built Me 163s was transferred to the *Erprobungsstelle der Luftwaffe*, Jesau, near Königsberg.

Shortly afterwards, EKdo 16 was ordered by Oberst Gordon Gollob, at the request of the *Kommandeur der Erprobungsstellen*, Oberst Petersen, to demonstrate the Me 163 at Rechlin before members of the *Jägerstab* on 12 and 13 June. The demonstration was to be witnessed by Reichsmarschall Göring, Generalfeldmarschall Milch and Japanese and Italian officials, who were beginning to show an interest in the Me 163. As the *Erprobungskommando* did not have any aircraft cleared for flight at that time, three aircraft were provided by 1./JG 400, the pilots, Hauptmann Rudolf Opitz and Oberleutnant Herbert Langer, being drawn from EKdo 16. The third aircraft was not to be flown but merely displayed for inspection.

Two of the aircraft, BV29 (GH+IH) and BV54 (GH+IW), were towed from Wittmundhafen to Rechlin, the first on 11 June piloted by Unteroffizier Kurt Schiebeler and the second on 13 June piloted by Feldwebel Rudolf Zimmermann. The third aircraft has not been identified but was probably a production aircraft built by Klemm. This aircraft might have already been delivered to Rechlin at an earlier date.

BV29 was flown by Opitz during a solo flying display at Rechlin on 12 June. During the climb-out after take-off, the engine flamed out at a height of 2,000 metres. After several attempts to restart the engine, Opitz decided to dump the remaining fuel and land. It was learned afterwards that very dirty *C-Stoff* had been delivered from Kiel and had blocked the *C-Stoff* filter fitted to the pressure control valve. New supplies of *C-Stoff* delivered overnight were also found to be dirty and had to be carefully filtered. Opitz and Langer successfully demonstrated their aircraft on 13 June, but then, in order to avoid getting in the way of an Me 262 which was also landing, Opitz decided to land close to the airfield's perimeter on a rough, fenced-off area. The skid dug into the soft ground and ploughed along the surface for about 80 metres, after which the aircraft somersaulted violently onto its back. *T-Stoff* leaked out of the fuselage tank and over him, and, according to EKdo 16's report, he suffered second degree burns to his left hand. Opitz recollects the event somewhat differently;

'I made a landing along the edge of the runway so as to leave it clear for the jet aircraft that were also being demonstrated that day. Unknown to us demonstration pilots, the anti-aircraft gunners, based at the airfield, had dug a ditch, running from their gun positions all the way to the runway, to give them some cover if they had to go to the runway in an emergency. So as I came almost to a stop, there was this ditch in front of me! Nobody had warned me. The aircraft dipped in and then went vertical, hesitated while it decided whether it should fall back or forwards. It decided to fall forwards and the canopy was crushed. Thankfully, it all happened in slow motion and I was not hurt at all. I just hung in my harness and waited for the soldiers to come and get me out – they were only nearby. They dug away as much as they could, so that I could slide out from under the broken canopy. But just as I began to slide out, a flame burst into the cockpit.

'I had uncoupled my harness and had fallen onto the ground beneath the canopy, but, unknown to me, there had been some leakage of hydrogen peroxide into the cockpit. So, of course, I made my exit in a hurry, but I was in flames – my hand was burning because the liquid had gone through the fabric of the glove, touched the skin and burst into flames. The fabric just caked, you couldn't get it off. Thankfully, however, the rescue people were right there and they had a fire truck with a hose which they turned on me. I had my best uniform on under the flight suit and the hydrogen peroxide had leaked all over my back – a fact of which I was not aware. My uniform, of course, was organic and, when they finally got the flight suit off me, they found that the arms and back of my uniform were burnt out but that the fuel had not got as far as my underwear. The quantity of water had meant that there was no damage to my skin. But I really was frightened.'

One of his rescuers was Kurt Schiebeler. He had accompanied the fire engine to the site, dug the hole under the canopy, smashed it, and pulled Opitz out of the cockpit, remarking, 'Herr Hauptmann, you were lucky!' At that moment Opitz' flying suit caught fire. Schiebeler reacted quickly and Opitz was doused with water from head to toe. Opitz was treated for his injuries in the Luftwaffe hospital at Wismar, joining Böhner who had been transferred there only a few days previously for treatment after his own accident.

The order forbidding operational sorties was eventually rescinded and Allied aircraft flying over the airfield were no longer immune. Wittmundhafen later came under scrutiny and an Allied reconnaissance flight made on 6 July noted the presence of seven Me 163s. That same day Rudolf Zimmermann recorded that he had made an unsuccessful attempt to intercept the enemy with BV59 GN+MB. On 7 July, Kurt Schiebeler flew two operational sorties with BV55 GH+IX, both unsuccessful. During the morning he had attempted to intercept a P-51 Mustang, and in the evening a P-38 Lightning. These were the last combat sorties to be flown by Me 163s at Wittmundhafen.

The transfer of 1./JG 400's aircraft to Brandis began about 10 July 1944 and the majority of the aircraft had been delivered there by 17 July. An advance party had already been sent to Brandis to prepare for the arrival of the Me 163s. Flight-worthy aircraft were towed to Brandis by Bf 110s, each of the towing aircraft carrying a spare undercarriage dolly for the Me 163 in case they were forced to make a landing en route. This precaution proved justified on at least one occasion during the move to Brandis. Increasingly bad weather and approaching darkness forced one pair of aircraft to land at the airfield at Borkheide, south of Berlin. Both aircraft made a safe landing on the airfield which was only 800 metres wide and 1,000 metres long! The two pilots, with the help of the Bf 110's flight engineer, managed to take off the next morning, the spare dolly remaining in Borkheide as a memento of the visit.

At about the same time, *Ergänzungsstaffel*/JG 400 under the command of Leutnant Franz Medicus was transferred from Bad Zwischenahn to Brandis.

The aircraft transferred to from Wittmundhafen to Brandis included BV48, BV50, BV52, BV55, BV56, White 1, White 2, White 3, White 4, and White 7 (BV62).

A small number of men, under the command of Oberleutnant Eberle, remained in Wittmundhafen to complete any outstanding work after the transfer. Interestingly, the Allies noted that one Me 163 had been seen at Wittmundhafen on 15 August, indicating that not all of the first squadron's aircraft had been transferred to Brandis in July.

The airfield, sited on low-lying land between the towns of Polenz and Leulitz, was built in 1934-35. It was officially named the *Fliegerhorst Waldpolenz* but it was also known as the *Flugplatz Brandis* and the US Army called it Polenz Airfield. Before and during the war, the airfield, code-named *Bickbeere* (Bilberry/Blueberry), was used for training aircrews and, from the beginning of 1943 onwards, it was also the home base of operational squadrons. From 1944 until the end of the war, it was used as a test centre for aircraft produced by Junkers Flugzeug- und Motorenwerke AG at Dessau.

The airfield was built initially for the use of *Blindflugschule* 1 to train pilots for the Luftwaffe in blind flying and navigation techniques. In the autumn of 1937, the navigation training activities were transferred to Anklam in northern Germany and blind flying training was retained at Brandis. On 15 October 1943, the school was redesignated *Flugzeugführerschule* 31. It was commanded by Oberst Paul Aue, a veteran of World War 1, who had served with distinction as *Offizierstellvertreter* in *Jagdstaffel* 10 of *Jagdgeschwader* 1, the squadron popularly known as Richthofen's Flying Circus.

Within three weeks of their arrival, 1./JG 400 was to be involved in the first of six major combats with the bombers and fighters of the Eighth Air Force. This took place on 28 July 1944 when USAAF forces drawn from the 1st and 3rd Bombardment Wings were sent to bomb Merseburg-Leuna and Leipzig-Taucha. Altogether 766 B-17s attacked the targets and 14 groups of P-38 Lightnings and P-51 Mustangs provided fighter escort. The USAAF Intops Summary recording the event noted: 'The most interesting development was the appearance of the jet-propelled Me 163, which however made no attacks either on the bombers or the fighters. Preliminary sightings indicate that six to eight of these aircraft were in the target area. Some were sighted by bomber crews at 0945 hrs and others at 1122 hrs by fighter pilots. Crews reported that the aircraft dove between the bomber formations without attacking, that they were highly manoeuvrable but unstable, yet faster, especially in a steep climb, than the P-51s which pursued them.'

359th FG (56 P-51s) saw five Me 163s at 0946 hrs. Col Avelin Tacon, who led the group, reported;

'I encountered two Me 163 fighters over Merseburg at 0946 hrs on 28 July 1944. My eight ship section was furnishing close support to a Combat Wing of B-17s that had just bombed Merseburg. The bombers were heading south at 24,000 feet and we were flying parallel to them about 1,000 yards to the east at 25,000 feet. Someone called in contrails high at six o'clock. I looked back and saw two contrails at about 32,000 feet about five miles away. I immediately called them to flight as jet propelled aircraft. There is no mistaking their contrails. It was white and very dense, as dense as a cumulus cloud and the same appearance except it was elongated. The two contrails I saw were about three-fourths of a mile long.

Col Avelin P Tacon Jr, who commanded the 359th FG on 28 July 1944 (*Avelin P Tacon*)

'We immediately dropped tanks and turned on gun switches while making a 180 degree turn back toward the bandits. It has since turned out in interrogation that there were five Me 163s, one flight of two, which I saw with jets on, and another flight of three without jets. The two I saw made a diving turn to the left, in good close formation, and started a six o'clock pass at the bombers. As soon as they turned they cut off their jets. We started a head-on overhead pass at them, getting between them and the rear of the bombers. When they were still about 3,000 yards from the bombers they saw us and made a slight turn to the left into us, and away from the bombers. Their bank was about 80 degrees in this turn, but they only changed course about 20 degrees. They did not attack the bombers. Their rate of roll appeared to be excellent, but radius of turn very large. I estimate, conservatively, they were doing between 500 and 600mph.

'Although I had seen them start their dive and watched them throughout their attack, I had no time to get my sights anywhere near them. Both ships, still in close formation and without jet propulsion, passed about 1,000 feet under us. I split-essed to try to follow them. As soon as they had passed under us one of them continued on in a 45 degrees dive and the other pulled up into the sun, which was about 50 or 60 degrees above the horizon. I glanced quickly up into the sun but could not see this one. When I looked back at the one that had continued the dive, approximately a second later, he was about five miles away down to perhaps 10,000 feet. Although I did not see it, the leader of my second flight reports that the aircraft that pulled up

Me 163B V53 Wk-Nr. 16310062 White 9, was flown by Unteroffizier Kurt Schiebeler on 4 August 1944. He made a test flight of 12 minutes late that evening. No satisfactory explanation has been found for the letter X added after the prototype number on the fin (*EN Archive*)

This photograph is believed to be one of a sequence taken for propaganda purposes in which various pilots were portrayed preparing for flight. The aircraft used on this occasion was Me 163B White 12; Feldwebel Siegfried Schubert is using the telephone (third from left). The field telephone resting on the wing was used to maintain contact with the pilot and the command post during take-off preparations (*JG 400 Archive*)

into the sun used his jet in short bursts. The flight leader described it as looking like he was blowing smoke rings. This ship disappeared and we don't know where he went.

'Their contrails could not be mistaken and looked very dense and white, somewhat like an elongated cumulus cloud some three quarters of a mile in length. My section turned 180 degree[s] back toward the enemy fighters, which included two with jets turned on and three in a glide without jets operating at the moment. These two pilots appeared very experienced but not aggressive.'

On 31 July 1944, 1./JG 400 reported that it had 16 Me 163s available of which only four were serviceable.

On 16 August 1944, the Eighth Air Force bombed Delitzsch, Halle, Böhlen and Schkeuditz, of which only the last three targets were within the range of Me 163s operating from Brandis. This force comprised 11 combat wings of 425 B-17s and six fighter groups of 48 P-47 Thunderbolts and 241 P-51s. The USAAF Intops Summary remarked;

'At 1050 hrs, a straggling B-17 of the combat wing dispatched against Halle was attacked by a single Me 163 about five miles west of Köthen, but the bomber successfully evaded. The high group of a second combat wing of the force, despatched against Böhlen, was attacked by two of six jet-propelled aircraft seen just after the turn from the target at 1059 hrs. Two passes were made by these aircraft, the first pass from 11 o'clock high, after which the enemy aircraft turned and came back on the tail of the formation from about 2,000 feet above. Aircraft came in with jets off and fired from cannon in wings. When

One of 305th BG's B-17s photographed after its return to Chelveston, Northamptonshire. The aircraft, XK-B, was piloted by Lt Charles Lavadiere and is reputed to have been damaged in an attack made by Leutnant Hartmut Ryll on 16 August 1944 although the damage to the B-17 is consistent with the gun camera photographs taken by Feldwebel Siegfried Schubert during an attack on a B-17 (*National Archives USA*)

they had approached to within 200 yards, they would turn on jets and break away so fast that it was impossible to trace them.'

These aircraft were identified as Me 163s.

Post-war research has revealed that the following USAAF aircraft were attacked during this bombing raid;

B-17 OR-N, 42-31636, *Outhouse Mouse* (1st Lt W Reese Mullins), 91st BG, aircraft attacked by Leutnant Hartmut Ryll.

B-17 XK-B (2nd Lt Charles Lavadiere), 305th BG, aircraft severely damaged in attack by Ryll, two gunners killed.

B-17 XK-D, 305th BG, attacked.

B-17 XK-G (1st Lt W E Jenks), 305th BG, attacked.

B-17 XK-H (2nd Lt D M Waltz), *Towering Titan*, 305th BG, attacked by Straznicky.

Donald M Waltz, the pilot of B-17 *Towering Titan*, recalled the mission;

'I was a 2nd Lt B-17 pilot in the 365th BS of the Eighth Air Forces 305th BG based at Chelveston, England. On the morning of 16 August, my crew and I were briefed for a daylight mission to bomb a German synthetic oil factory south-west of the city of Leipzig. It was only our fourth combat mission. This was considered a deep penetration mission because of Leipzig's location in Germany. We carried the maximum gross weight of fuel and bombs. Our 12-aeroplane squadron – all B-17s – was divided into three four-plane elements. I was assigned to fly off the squadron leader, Lt W E Jenks, left wing in the fourship lead element. I think 2nd Lt Charles Lavadiere was assigned the slot position.

'Our bomb group had been briefed for the previous ten days on the possibility of attack by a new German "jet" fighter aeroplane – the

Me 163. At our early morning briefing on 16 August, our Group Intelligence Officer again described the Me 163. He said the aeroplane was in early production – not too many in operation so we were "unlikely to see the Me 163 on this Leipzig mission".

'He further indicated that if we did encounter the Me 163, we would have no problem with aircraft recognition, "it will be the fastest aircraft any of us have seen." I recall that mission being long and rough. Had the German industry been able to produce more of them in the Fall of 1944, the air war over Europe could have been a tougher place for the USAAF and RAF.'

2nd Lt Paul Davidson was navigator on board *Towering Titan*. He wrote in his diary;

'The skies over Germany were black with planes. Fire in the whole of south-eastern Germany could be seen for miles. Flak was intense and accurate between the IP [Intercept Point] and the target. We received seven holes in our ship, one of which missed an engine by two inches. It could have been fatal. At 1056 hrs, a jet-propelled Me 163 made a pass at our aeroplane from six o'clock high. Our tail turret gunner S/Sgt Howard Kaysen (we called him "Red") gave the enemy a long burst all the way in. "Red" was our best gunner. The Me 163 came within 50 yards and then peeled off as Red plastered him. The Me 163 went into a dive trailing black smoke.'

Kaysen claimed the Me 163 flown by Feldwebel Herbert Straznicky of 1./JG 400, who was wounded in the attack, baled out and was

The crew of B-17 *Towering Titan* photographed at Chelveston, England, in August 1944. Front row, from left to right: T/Sgt Paul Kennedy (radio operator), T/Sgt Joe Kutskel (flight engineer), S/Sgt Howard Kaysen (tail gunner), S/Sgt Marvin Dennis (ball turret gunner). Back row, from left to right: S/Sgt Collin Lyerla (waist gunner), Captain Don Waltz (pilot), Captain Paul Davidson (navigator), 1st Lt Sam Stempler (bombardier), 1st Lt John Keysor (co-pilot) (*Don Waltz*)

The crew of *Outhouse Mouse*: kneeling, left to right – T/Sgt James R Knaub (radio operator), S/Sgt Kenneth I Blackburn (ball turret gunner), Sgt Joe V Cullen (assistant engineer and waist gunner), S/Sgt Robert D Loomis (armourer and waist gunner), Sgt Gordon D Smith (tail gunner, replaced on 16 August mission by S/Sgt M D Barker) and T/Sgt Carl A Dickson (engineer and top turret gunner). Standing, left to right – Flt Off Raymond Nassimbeni (co-pilot who was replaced on 16 August mission by 2nd Lt Forrest P Drewery), 1st Lt W Reese 'Moon' Mullins (pilot), 2nd Lt John O'Connor (navigator and nose gunner) and Flt Off O V Chaney (bombardier and chin turret gunner) *(James R Knaub and George Oldenwaller)*

initially posted as killed in action. The Me 163 exploded on impact with the ground.

Elsewhere, B-17 *Outhouse Mouse* of the 91st BG, piloted by 1st Lt W Reese Walker Mullins, was straggling behind the main bomber force having turned for home from the Leuna synthetic fuel plant. *Outhouse Mouse* had been damaged earlier during an attack by Fw 190s from IV.*Sturm*/JG 3. With two damaged superchargers and wounded crew members, the aircraft was in bad shape. At 1045 hrs, Leutnant Hartmut Ryll of 1./JG 400 made a gliding attack in his Me 163 from six o'clock high, his cannon firing as it approached. Mullins began 'rocking the ship up down' in an urgent evasive action. 'We started skidding back and forth,' 2nd Lt Forrest P Drewery, the co-pilot recounted to an American newspaper. Ryll was unable to score any hits on the lumbering but weaving bomber. Ryll's attack, however, did not go unobserved.

Lt Col John B Murphy, 370th FS, 359th FG, recorded in his enemy encounter report of 16 August 1944;

'I was escorting our bombers southeast of Leipzig at 27,000 feet when I noticed a contrail climbing rapidly up toward the bombers from behind and port side. I recognised the contrail as being produced by a jet-propelled aircraft because of its speed. Due to its speed and altitude advantage I knew I could not overtake him, but noticed a straggling B-17 to the starboard at 25,000 feet which was headed north and east of Leipzig all alone, and I headed toward him, thinking that he

probably would be attacked. The jettie contrail ceased about 500 yards from the bomber, and from that point on, I kept him in sight as I would any other aircraft. He passed through the bombers and down to the straggling B-17 and arrived there before I could; however, I wasn't far behind and was overtaking.

'After he passed the B-17, he seemed to level off, and as I closed on him, I opened fire from about 1,000 feet and held it until I overshot. I scored a few hits on the left side of the fuselage. I pulled up to the left as sharply as I could to prevent overshooting and getting out in front of him and lost sight of both him and my wingman. My wingman, Lt Jones, reported that the jettie flipped over on his back in a half roll, and as he did so, he scored a sufficient number of hits in the canopy to destroy him. As Jones tried to follow him through on his dive, Jones blacked out.

'When I completed my sharp chandelle turn to the left, I saw another jettie off to my left and Jones farther off and lower to my right. I started down on this one, which was making rather shallow diving turns to the left. I think I must have turned with him through two turns before overtaking him. I realised that I was going to overtake him rapidly too, but I held my fire to an estimated 750 feet and held a continuous burst, seeing continuous strikes the full length of the fuselage. Parts began falling off, followed by a big explosion and more parts falling off. I could smell a strange chemical fume in my cockpit as I followed through the smoke from the explosion. It seemed to me that a large chunk of the

B-17 *Outhouse Mouse* (s/n 42-31636) of the 91st BG was piloted by 1st Lt W Reese Walker Mullins, and was one of the first Eighth Air Force Flying Fortresses to be attacked by Me 163s when Leutnant Hartmut Ryll of 1./JG 400 made a gliding approach towards the bomber from six o'clock high during a mission to Halle, Böhlen and Schkeuditz *(James R Knaub and George Oldenwaller)*

fuselage from the canopy on back just popped off with the explosion. I followed him part of the way down, and my intent was to follow him down until he hit, but I saw another jettie at my same altitude about two miles off and decided against it. Being by myself and low on gas, I did not attack this other jet, but headed home.

'My first impression when I saw the jet was that I was standing still. It seemed hopeless to try to attempt to overtake them, but my actions were prompted by a curiosity to get as close to them as possible. I believe that will be the reaction of every pilot that comes in contact with them. Another thing that is very noticeable is that their speed varies considerably, but it's hard to realise this until you find yourself rapidly overtaking them.

'It's my impression that they would be particularly blind from below and from the sides due to the size of the wing span.

'I wish it to be considered that there is the possibility that the two aircraft claimed as destroyed could be only one, but I feel it very improbable due to the manoeuvres and positions of the two.

'I claim one (1) Me 163 destroyed in air and one (1) Me 163 damaged in air.'

Lt Cyril W Jones Jr also of 370th FS, who was flying with Murphy, recorded in his report;

'I was flying White Two when White Leader called in a jettie making a pass at the bombers we were escorting. White Leader said to keep an eye on the enemy aircraft. We were about two miles from the bomber formation, and the jet aircraft was on the other side of the bombers. White Leader started a turn toward one bomber straggler which looked as if it might be a target for the jet aircraft; as we started the turn, I noticed three other contrails similar to the one White Leader had called in. They were going through another formation of bombers. I could see no aircraft at the end of the trails, but decided they must be other jet aircraft. I did not try to watch them longer and concentrated on following my leader.

According to the combat report written by Lt Col John B Murphy (right), he damaged the Me 163 flown by Leutnant Hartmut Ryll (far right) before turning to attack another Me 163 on 16 August 1944 (his wingman, Lt Cyril W Jones, completed the destruction of the Me 163) (*John B Murphy*)

Leutnant Hartmut Ryll, 1./JG 400, seated in the cockpit of his Me 163. Ryll was the first of JG 400's pilots to be killed in combat. The identity of the aircraft which Ryll was flying at the time he was killed is not known, the personnel loss report (*Namentliche Verlustmeldung*) quotes an incomplete *Werknummer* (*JG 400 Archive*)

'The enemy aircraft that we were trying to intercept completed his run on the formation of bombers, passing through them and heading for the straggler. He completed the run on the straggler and he passed about 500 yards in front and to the starboard of the bomber when we overtook them. White Leader was about 1,000 feet ahead of me and about 500 feet above me on the final approach. I saw White Leader fire, and strikes appeared on the tail of the enemy aircraft. White Leader broke away, and I continued in, the jet aircraft split-essed, and I followed him. I fired a short burst with a three-radii lead and observed no hits. I increased the lead and fired again. The entire canopy seemed to dissolve on the enemy aircraft which I had identified as an Me 163. I closed very fast and broke behind him. As I passed behind the enemy aircraft, I hit his wash and did a half turn. While recovering, I blacked out and lost sight of the Me 163. I recovered at 14,000 feet after starting the attack at 23,000 feet. The pilot was surely killed when the bullets entered his canopy, and I claim one Me 163 destroyed. I could not find my leader and being low on gas, I returned home.

'While the Me 163 has its jet in operation, it would be impossible for the P-51 to overtake it, but with the jet off or expended, it seems to be slower than the P-51. It is difficult to judge the speed of the jet aircraft with its power off, and its speed seems to change very quickly. I had no chance to manoeuvre with the Me 163 beyond my firing point and could not very well determine its manoeuvrability. It climbs at an almost vertical angle, faster than the conventional aircraft can cruise in level flight; that is, with its power on. It also has very great acceleration with its power on and a fast gliding speed immediately after using its power.

'I claim one (1) Me 163 destroyed in air.'

Leutnant Hartmut Ryll of 1./JG 400, was killed in action over Bad Lausick east-south-east of Leipzig. He was flying an Me 163B, which in the official loss record, lists the incomplete Wk-Nr. 163100??. The aircraft crashed vertically in *Planquadrat* LF4/LF6 at 1052 hrs.

2. STAFFEL/ JAGDGESCHWADER 400

Official records indicate that this squadron was to be established at Oranienburg as early as 27 March 1944 and remain there until 22 July. The same records indicate that 2./JG 400 arrived at Venlo before the end of July. Statistical records kept by the *Luftflotte Reich* concerning squadron strengths state that the squadron had 12 aircraft but was not operational on 10 April. After that date the statistics do not mention the whereabouts of 2./JG 400, apart from stating that the squadron was no longer at Oranienburg. None of the squadron's pilots recalls any of these events. Oranienburg was probably an assembly point for ground personnel destined to join the squadron and was probably also where they received technical training.

According to an order signed by Hans-Georg von Seidel, *Generalquartiermeister der Luftwaffe*, 2./JG 400 was established on 6 April 1944. The order was to be implemented immediately and the squadron was to be placed under the command of *Luftgaukommando* III.

According to Hauptmann Böhner, JG 400's second squadron was established under his command at Bad Zwischenahn at the beginning of July 1944. The squadron's pilots included Oberleutnant Joachim Bialucha, Leutnant Günter Andreas, Rolf Schlegel and Heinz Schubert, Oberfeldwebel Jakob Bollenrath, Fritz Husser and Fritz Kelb, Feldwebel Horst Rolly, and Unteroffiziere Manfred Eisenmann, Rolf Glogner and Ernst Schelper. They were joined by Leutnant Dorsel, who became the squadron's *Nachrichtenoffizier*.

2./JG 400 was equipped with aircraft produced by Klemm, the majority of the Me 163s being delivered from Jesau. During the second half of August the squadron also began receiving aircraft completed at

Hauptmann Otto Böhner and aircraft at Venlo, August 1944. Böhner gained the first of his pilot's licences in the period 1934-35. He enlisted in the Luftwaffe at Oldenburg, afterwards joining the fighter school at Werneuchen. In April 1937, he transferred as Leutnant to 4./JG 334 (later renamed JG 53) at Mannheim and served in the French campaign, claiming three aircraft destroyed. In October 1940, Böhner was appointed *Staffelkapitän* of 6./JG 53 and flew escort fighter duties during the Battle of Britain, served with his squadron in Sicily and, after March 1942, served as a technical officer with JG 53 in North Africa. He transferred to EKdo 16 at Peenemünde in August 1943, shortly before that unit was moved to Bad Zwischenahn. In January 1944, he was made technical officer, EKdo 16, after the death of Oberleutnant Josef 'Joschi' Pöhs. Böhner was appointed *Staffelführer* of 1./JG 400 at Wittmundhafen after the accident to Olejnik on 21 April. He joined 2./JG 400 at Venlo in July as *Staffelkapitän*, after a period of convalescence following his own accident at Wittmundhafen on 28 May (*Otto Böhner*)

Leutnant Heinz Schubert, who was put in command of 2./JG 400 while Hauptmann Böhner recovered from his injuries sustained at Wittmundhafen (*JG 400 Achive*)

Oranienburg, to where final assembly and testing had been transferred from Jesau, between 4 and 24 August. All of the aircraft were delivered by rail.

Andreas and Bialucha were sent to Venlo at the end of June to make preparations for the arrival of 2./JG 400, and Hauptmann Böhner returned to Bad Zwischenahn at the beginning of July after a stay in hospital because of head injuries he had sustained in an accident on 28 May while testing BV57 at Wittmundhafen. On that occasion, he had been making an approach to land his still partly fuelled aircraft when the linkage deploying one of the landing flaps had broken. He had had no time to retract the other flap and only just enough time to make a forced landing in a cornfield, the surface of which had appeared to be relatively smooth. The aircraft had bounced into the air before finally coming to rest and after Böhner's head had made contact with the gunsight. Leutnant Heinz Schubert had been nominated to command 2./JG 400 in Böhner's absence. Böhner, however, had still not fully recovered from his injuries and he was once again sent for treatment. He rejoined his squadron at Venlo at the end of July.

The squadron's personnel transferred to Venlo about the middle of July. At that time they still had no aircraft and it was not until shortly after Böhner's return to the squadron that they received their first Me 163. The first few weeks at Venlo were occupied with training, the squadron sharing the airfield with *Staffeln* from I./NJG 1 and III./KG 3 and *Erprobungskommando* 410. Hauptmann Böhner flew the first Me 163 to arrive. He recalled;

'The airfield is slightly elevated, and when one tries to land from a particular direction, from the west, one gets an updraft from the dunes and the aircraft is pushed up and the landing strip all of a sudden is too short. That happened to me. I overshot the runway. Nothing much happened. The aircraft was a total loss but I was fine.'

On 26 July, Feldwebel Rolly crashed during a training flight, the aircraft, BQ+UL (Wk-Nr. 440009) was damaged.

On 12 August 1944, Joachim Bialucha was killed under tragic circumstances. Andreas recalls;

'We were in our quarters relaxing after our evening meal. At 2100 hrs, as Officer of the Watch, I began to patrol the airfield. At 2300 hrs, just as I was passing the main gate, I noticed Bialucha with his bicycle waiting there. The guard, not knowing him, had refused to let him through. He was pleased to see me and asked me if I would allow him through so that he could take a short cut across the airfield to visit his wife who was living on the German side of the border near Kaldenkirchen.

'I returned to my quarters and was just beginning to fall asleep when I heard the telephone ringing in Hauptmann Böhner's room, which was next to mine. His answer as to whether he was missing an Oberleutnant was no. The caller said that there had been a fatal accident involving someone riding one of the *Staffel*'s bicycles. Since Bialucha was the only member of our squadron with this rank I realised something was amiss. I went to Bialucha's quarters and discovered that he was not there and concluded that he must still be somewhere on his bicycle. Böhner, Schubert and I drove over to the scene of the accident, where we found Bialucha. He had ridden across the airfield and, in the dark, had collided

Otto Böhner prepares to take off at Venlo in Klemm-built aircraft Wk-Nr. 440014. Aircraft from the batch were assigned call signs BQ+UD to BQ+UW; Wk-Nr. 440014 corresponds to BQ+UQ but the aircraft was never painted with this call sign (*EN Archive*)

with the propeller of a nightfighter being towed by a tractor. He had then fallen in front of one of the aircraft's undercarriage wheels.'

The airfield at Venlo was attacked several times, Fritz Husser being of the opinion that this was because of the He 111s stationed there which were used to mount attacks with the V1s they carried. He recalls that at least one of the aircraft was blown to pieces while it was being loaded with a V1 (these He 111s were flown by III./KG 3). Böhner, however, believes that these attacks were made to hinder nightfighter operations and it was for this reason that Oberst Gollob had visited Venlo's ground control command post on one occasion.

The first major attack on the airfield was made on 15 August 1944 by B-17s of the USAAF's 390th BG under the command of Col L W Dolan. The attack was led by Lt Maher and over one thousand 100-lb general purpose bombs were dropped on the airfield.

It is not known exactly when the squadron made its first operational sortie, only that it was unsuccessful. Five aircraft were scrambled. Böhner recalls that the sortie took place one or two days after Feldwebel Siegfried Schubert, who served with 1./JG 400 at Brandis, had claimed a bomber, one of a force of B-17s which had attacked Böhlen on 16 August. Andreas, Bollenrath, Schelper, Kelb and Heinz Schubert participated in 2./JG 400's first attack.

On 2 September, Hauptmann Böhner was informed by the *Fliegerhorst-Kommandant* that the airfield's installations would be destroyed the next day because the enemy was approaching. Since the Me 163 could not simply be flown away, Böhner ordered the aircraft to be towed overland to Wesel. The wings were disconnected from the fuselages and the disassembled aircraft were prepared for transportation that night. The squadron took three days to reach its destination, bivouacking in the woods en route. The aircraft were towed on their undercarriage dollies and the refuelling bowsers were fitted with makeshift racks to accommodate the squadron's equipment. The wheels of the dollies had to be greased regularly as they had not been designed for this form of transportation.

The progress of the convoy with its '*Wunderwaffe*' was watched in silent amazement by villagers as it made its way to Wesel. There, the squadron hid in a wood until they received an order from Oberst Gollob to entrain for Brandis. The airfield at Venlo was heavily shelled by US forces on 3 September.

Leutnant Günter Andreas was sent to prepare for the arrival of 2./JG 400 at Brandis. The day after he arrived there, an Obergefreiter belonging to the squadron reported to him that two railway wagons filled with military goods were standing in the airfield's sidings and needed to be unloaded. The train arrived at Brandis before the *Staffel*;

Before moving to Brandis during the first week of September 1944, aircraft of 2./JG 400 based at Venlo were scrambled on 27 August 1944 to intercept RAF Halifax and Lancaster bombers en route to bomb an oil refinery at Homberg, 12km northeast of Düsseldorf. The Me 163s were intercepted by Spitfires of No 303 Sqn RAF led by Wg Cdr John Checketts (below) which were escorting the bomber group. Checketts' aircraft was attacked by one of the rocket fighters, but the New Zealand ace – who would end the war with 15 confirmed victories and the DFC and DSO – managed to evade being shot down. The photograph to the left shows one of the Me 163s climbing towards a Spitfire escorting the bomber formation (*EN Archive*)

Hauptmann Böhner and the rest of 2./JG 400 arrived at Brandis two days later.

It transpired that two soldiers, who had taken the goods destined for the squadron from Brussels to Venlo, had arrived amidst the chaos of the squadron's departure from Venlo and, naturally, had not been able to find anyone in authority who would accept their delivery. They had then reported to Böhner who had recommended that they also should attempt to make their way to Brandis. The two soldiers had accomplished this brilliantly. They had bribed the engine driver and the train's personnel with some of the goods (they had more than enough!) and managed to arrive at Brandis before the *Staffel*. The unloading of the goods – among which were very large quantities of cognac, liqueurs and wines – proved difficult as the squadron had not been allocated any room for storage. Somehow room was found and the squadron thereafter quickly became a favourite.

Feldwebel Hans Hoever later recalled this move;

'I was transferred from *Luftnachrichten-Regiment* 211 to 2./JG 400 under the command of Hauptmann Otto Böhner in August 1944. At that time the *Staffel* was based in Venlo. My platoon commander, Leutnant Dorsel, and I had received orders to establish a fighter operations command post for the Me 163 close to the control tower at Venlo airport in the same way that we had done over the years for the nightfighters of NJG 1 at Venlo. This was my first contact with the new aircraft and their crews and I was able to build up a good working relationship with Hauptmann Böhner, although I, as a signals officer, was probably regarded by him almost as an outsider. We received orders to transfer our unit to Brandis soon after we had been subjected to a number of bombing raids.

'At the suggestion of Hauptmann Böhner we also took this opportunity to "redirect" all the supplies and goods belonging to NJG 1, which had been abandoned and were piled up at the railway station, to Brandis. We only discovered what a haul we had made when we opened up the two goods wagons. The large quantity of alcohol we found was put to good use and, needless to say, many parties were held. I later paid the proceeds from the sale of the goods, amounting to about 53,000 RM, into the savings bank at Brandis.

'Leutnant Dorsel and I set up the radar station in Brandis. This was located to the left and right of a road leading from the airfield to the town itself. As far as I can remember, the radar for the Me 163 was set up one kilometre to the north of the western end of the runway. I spent much of my free time watching the Me 163 take-off, fly and land, whereby I got to know many of the pilots.'

Aircraft believed to have been transferred from Venlo to Brandis in September bore the *Werknummern* 440003 (BQ+UF), 440006 (BQ+UI), 440007 (BQ+UJ), 440013 (BQ+UP), 440014 (BQ+UQ) and 440015 (BQ+UR).

An armoured infantry task force, formed from the US 35th Infantry Division and placed under the command of Col Bernard A Byrne, captured the airfield at Venlo on 1 March 1945! Soon afterwards the 852nd Aviation Engineer Battalion, commanded by Lt Col Arlong Hazen, moved into the airfield to begin repairs. There they found several Me 163s buried under the rubble of the hangars.

COLOUR PLATES

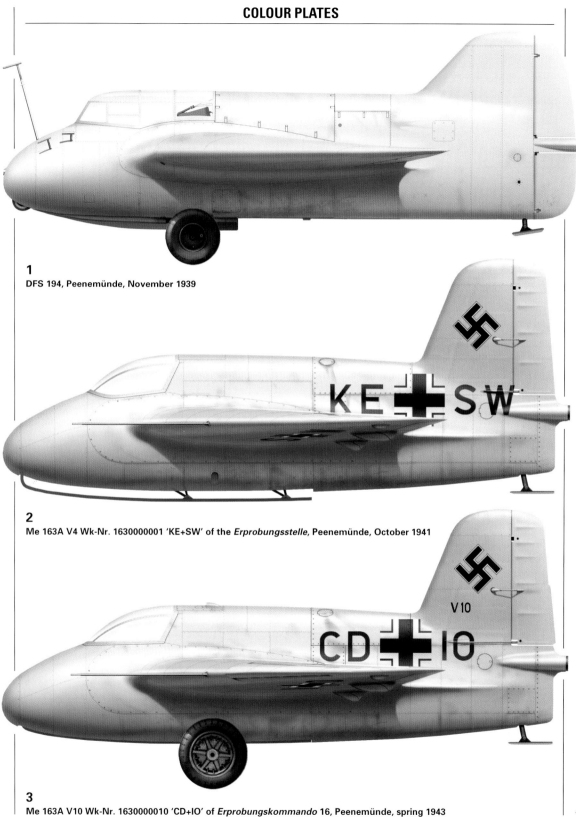

1
DFS 194, Peenemünde, November 1939

2
Me 163A V4 Wk-Nr. 1630000001 'KE+SW' of the *Erprobungsstelle*, Peenemünde, October 1941

3
Me 163A V10 Wk-Nr. 1630000010 'CD+IO' of *Erprobungskommando* 16, Peenemünde, spring 1943

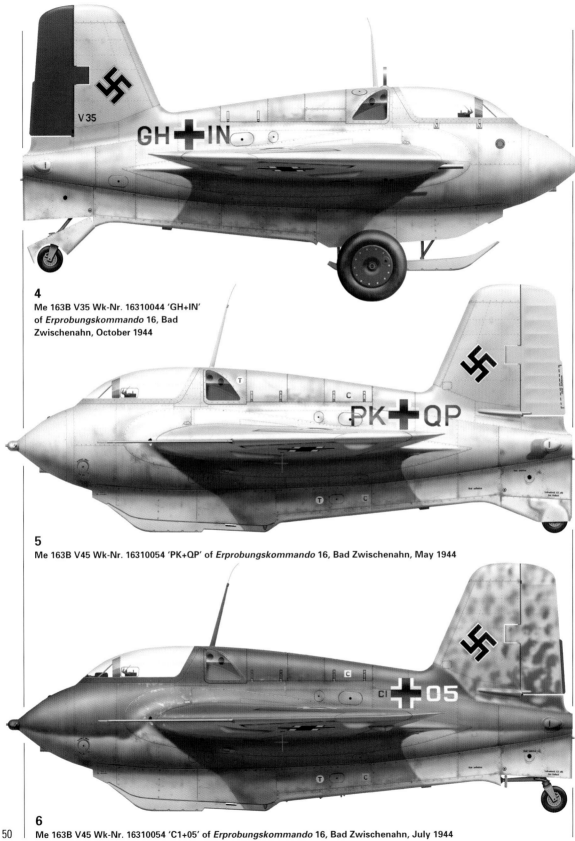

4
Me 163B V35 Wk-Nr. 16310044 'GH+IN'
of *Erprobungskommando* 16, Bad
Zwischenahn, October 1944

5
Me 163B V45 Wk-Nr. 16310054 'PK+QP' of *Erprobungskommando* 16, Bad Zwischenahn, May 1944

6
Me 163B V45 Wk-Nr. 16310054 'C1+05' of *Erprobungskommando* 16, Bad Zwischenahn, July 1944

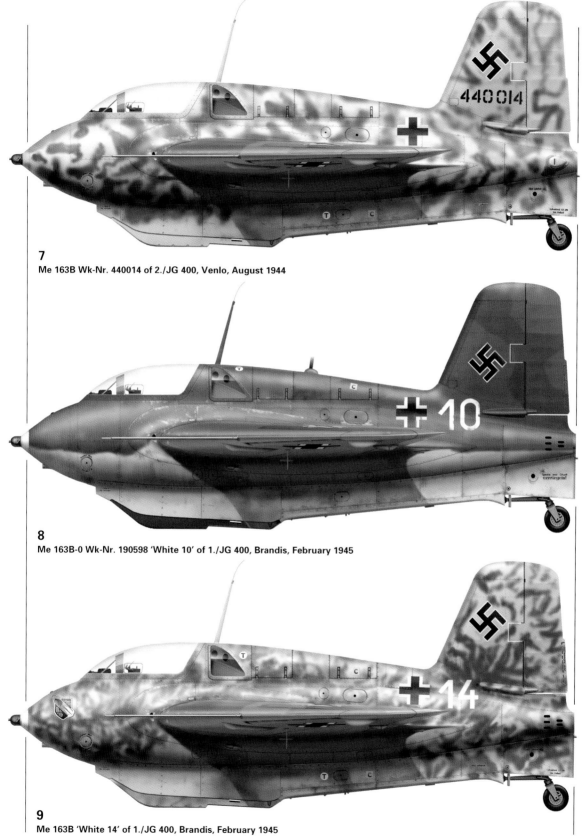

7
Me 163B Wk-Nr. 440014 of 2./JG 400, Venlo, August 1944

8
Me 163B-0 Wk-Nr. 190598 'White 10' of 1./JG 400, Brandis, February 1945

9
Me 163B 'White 14' of 1./JG 400, Brandis, February 1945

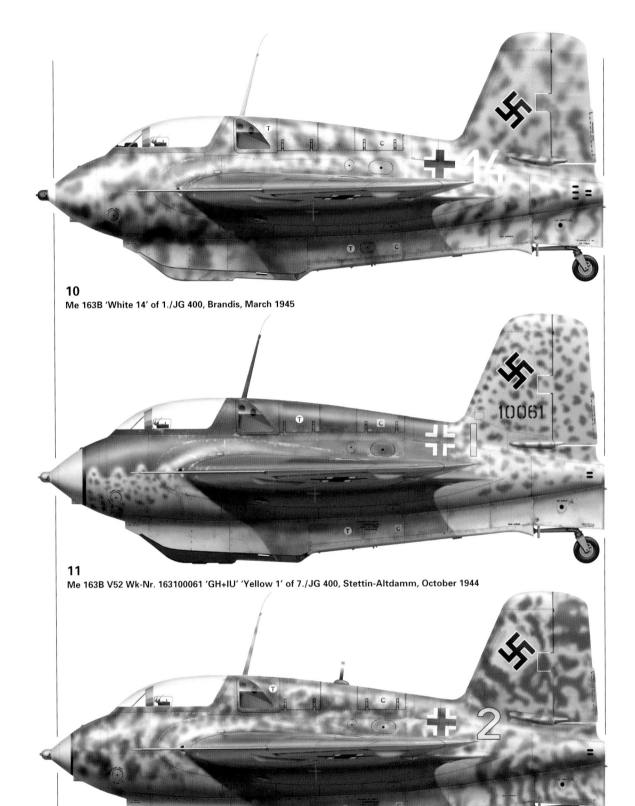

10
Me 163B 'White 14' of 1./JG 400, Brandis, March 1945

11
Me 163B V52 Wk-Nr. 163100061 'GH+IU' 'Yellow 1' of 7./JG 400, Stettin-Altdamm, October 1944

12
Me 163B 'Yellow 2' of 7./JG 400, Husum, May 1945

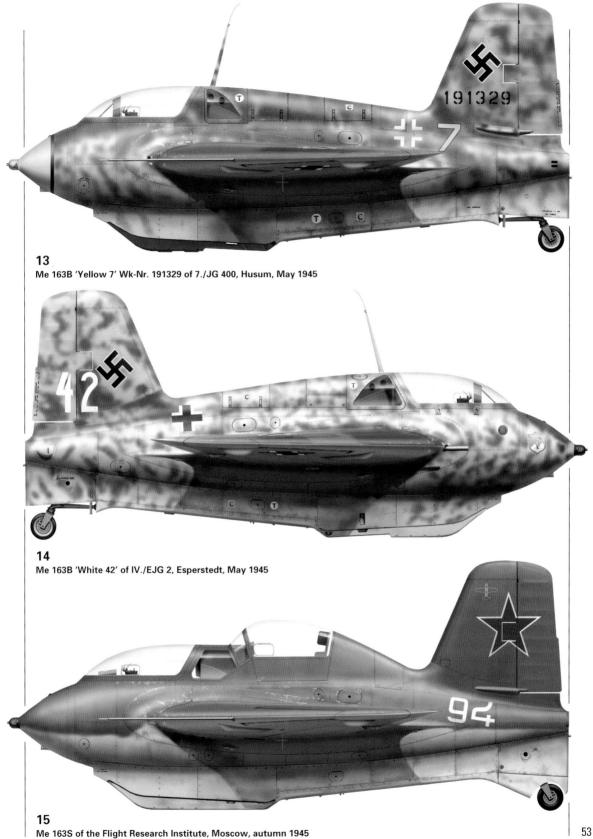

13
Me 163B 'Yellow 7' Wk-Nr. 191329 of 7./JG 400, Husum, May 1945

14
Me 163B 'White 42' of IV./EJG 2, Esperstedt, May 1945

15
Me 163S of the Flight Research Institute, Moscow, autumn 1945

Badge 1
1./JG 400

Badge 2
IV./EJG 2

I. GRUPPE/ JAGDGESCHWADER 400

The numbers of aircraft involved in the daylight attacks carried out by the US Eighth Air Force against targets in and around Merseburg, although totalling hundreds on any one day, were in fact only a small proportion of the total number of aircraft attacking Germany on that day, many of which were intercepted and destroyed by Bf 109s, Fw 190s and anti-aircraft fire before they reached their targets. In general, Me 163s were scrambled only when German radar confirmed that the bombers were heading towards the area around Merseburg, and then only when the bombers were about 50km from their target.

The Me 163s of I./JG 400 were scrambled during major USAAF attacks up until 2 November 1944. After this period, although the USAAF continued to attack Merseburg and nearby strategic targets, the first group's aircraft were not scrambled to meet these mass attacks but only occasionally attempted to intercept, sometimes successfully, lone Allied reconnaissance aircraft.

In a memorandum dated 19 August 1944 describing the Me 163 and its performance, distributed by the office of the *General der Jagdflieger*, Adolf Galland, at Berlin-Kladow, the name *Komet* was used, firstly in connection with its performance as a *Kometenjäger* and secondly with regard to the location of a training school then at Aalborg which was named *Kometen-Waffenschule*. No other document has been found which refers to the Me 163 by the name *Komet*, and it is not known when this name was officially allotted or first used.

Another memorandum sent the same day, also from the office of the *General der Jagdflieger*, outlined the status of JG 400 at that time;

On 19 August 1944, Generalmajor Adolf Galland, the *General der Jagdflieger*, issued a comprehensive resumé of the status of JG 400 and referred to the Me 163 as a '*Kometjäger*' but it is not known when this name was officially allocated or first used (*EN Archive*)

Stab I./JG 400	In the process of being established. Personnel available. To be based at Brandis.
1./JG 400	Squadron base Brandis. Formation complete and deployed; all personnel available. Fifteen aircraft available of which nine were delivered in July.
2./JG 400	Squadron base Venlo. Formation complete; all personnel available. Allotted eight Me 163Bs.
3./JG 400	Squadron base Stargard. In the process of being established. Trained personnel available. Aircraft not yet available; to be allotted aircraft from the Augsburg [sic] production line delivered in September.
4./JG 400	Application made for its formation. Personnel available; in training.
Erg.St./JG 400	Already formed. All personnel available. Training will follow guidelines currently laid down by the

General der Fliegerausbildung. [The guidelines required 35 qualified pilots per month. They were to complete their training with the *Ergänzungsstaffel*. Those who did not qualify, or who made a request to do so, were to be returned to their previous units.]

Schleppstaffel/JG 400   Application made for its formation. To be formed at Kölleda, where the Bf 110 is currently being modified for towing purposes. An application for personnel must be made to L-Wehr [the local recruitment centre].

In August, Me 163Bs were delivered from Klemm's production line. These aircraft had initially been sent to Jesau for final assembly and acceptance testing before they were delivered to JG 400 but in August this work was transferred to Oranienburg near Berlin. At about the same time, Klemm and Junkers began working together to produce the aircraft, Junkers officially taking over full responsibility for the production of Me 163s on 1 September 1944.

The order for the formation of 4./JG 400 was issued by the OKL on 4 September 1944. The *Staffel* was to have a strength of 12 Me 163Bs and to be supplemented by four Bf 110Gs and their crews for towing duties.

During take-offs, attempts to intercept enemy aircraft and landings, there were a number of incidents and accidents resulting from technical defects and the handling of the Me 163. One such event was later recalled by Leutnant Hans Bott, 1./JG 400, as told to him by Oberleutnant Franz Rösle, 1./JG 400. The incident took place on or around 20 August 1944. Bott maintains, however, that their targets were three or four P-38 Lightnings and not, as remembered by Rösle, a single Mosquito. Rösle;

'It was a beautiful summer evening, half-an-hour before dusk. Leutnant Bott and I were on stand-by in our aircraft ready to scramble, although neither of us thought we would be flying that evening. Suddenly, we received a message over our headsets that an enemy reconnaissance aircraft was approaching at 8,000-9,000 metres. Our excitement mounted. A few seconds later, we saw the contrail before us. Neither of us thought of the dangers we might have to face during the take-off itself. The order came to scramble.

'I immediately started the turbine-driven fuel pump, waited for the pressure to build up and then pushed the throttle to full thrust. The aircraft lifted off at 350km/h after a take-off run of 1,500 metres. I kept my eyes on the contrail and jettisoned the undercarriage dolly. I then pulled the Me 163 into a climb of 60-70 degrees at a speed of 100-150 metres-per-second and headed for the target. A few seconds later, I had reached a height of 8,000 metres, where I levelled off and saw a Mosquito ahead of me. I pressed the arming button and could clearly see the Mosquito in my gunsight. I was only three kilometres away from him, when, suddenly, my aircraft reared up vertically and the control column was torn out of my hands. I cast a glance at my speed indicator and saw that I was flying at 1,050km/h! A moment later, the aircraft pitched down and began to dive, and I was able to regain control.

While flying the Me 163B with 1./JG 400 at Brandis, Leutnant Hans Bott suffered two rocket engine flame-outs during the take-off phase at a height of 200 to 500 metres but on both occasions managed to make emergency landings. During another take-off, the rocket engine quit when rolling over the ground at a speed of 50-80km/h. He climbed out of the cockpit, rolled over the wing and jumped off the aircraft, suffering concussion and fracturing an ankle in the process. The Me 163B continued rolling in a wide circle and came to a halt without any damage. He had one confirmed and one possible aerial victory when flying the Me 163B. He transferred with Major Wolfgang Späte to JG 7, Prague-Ruzyne, but the situation there did not allow him to be trained to fly the Me 262 (*JG 400 Archive*)

This panorama was taken from a film produced by the Ufa studio in Berlin, who were at Brandis between around 21 August and 9 September 1944 to make a propaganda film of Me 163 operations. The Me 163s on the apron at the eastern end of the runway are covered with tarpaulins to protect them from a downpour of rain, puddles from which had not dried up at the time the film was made (*EN Archive*)

'Shortly afterwards, I realised that, in my excitement, I had forgotten to throttle back the engine. I later found out that the same thing had happened to Leutnant Bott. We had both flown above 1,000km/h and had experienced the effects of compressibility as we approached the speed of sound. This incident was nothing in comparison to what happened to me on my next sortie (on 13 September).'

On 24 August 1944, the Eighth Air Force bombed Merseburg and also Kölleda and Weimar. The Intops Summary of the mission recorded;

Leutnant Gustav Korff was instrumental in developing the radar-and radio-guided interception tactics used to direct Me 163s to their targets. He is seen here in the operational command post with Fräulein Linnig, who served as an officer with the Luftwaffe's Auxiliary Signals Corps (*Günther F Heise*)

Feldwebel Siegfried Schubert who scored the first of JG 400's victories on 16 August 1944. He was to lose his life during take-off for combat when his aircraft flamed out on 7 October (*JG 400 Archive*)

'One combat wing of the 2nd Force was attacked at 1205 hrs by three Me 163s northeast of Merseburg between the IP and the target and additional attacks were made by two single Me 163s southeast of Leipzig (185 B-17s attacked the oil refinery at Merseburg and ten B-17s attacked secondary targets in the area near Leipzig).'

According to post-war research conducted by Jeff Ethell the following USAAF aircraft were attacked during this bombing raid;

B-17 (Lt Koehler), 92nd BG, aircraft severely damaged in attack by Feldwebel Siegfried Schubert. This aircraft was lost en route to England.
B-17 (1st Lt Robert Swift), 92nd BG, attacked.
B-17 (1st Lt Harold H Baird), 92nd BG, attacked.
B-17 (JW-N, 1st Lt Lloyd G Henry), 92 BG, attacked.
B-17 (PY-R, 2nd Lt Steve Nagy), 92nd BG, shot down by Feldwebel Schubert's wingman, Leutnant Bott.
B-17 (2nd Lt C E Harris), 305th BG, attacked.
B-17 (KY-A, 2nd Lt P M Dabney), 305th BG, shot down.
B-17 (WF-B, 2nd Lt K H Dubanowich), 305th BG, attacked.
B-17 (WF-D, 1st Lt C E Frisby), 305th BG, attacked.
B-17 (WF-L, 2nd Lt E E Henry), 305th BG, attacked.

The crew of B-17 *Spare Parts* of the 305th BG in front of their aircraft, so-named because the crew was formed of 'replacements'! On 24 August 1944, *Spare Parts* encountered an Me 163 at close range. Pilot Eugene Arnold Jr recalled 'The German pilot and I were staring at each other … I told the gunners to fire at him (even my guys couldn't miss at that range)…' Seen here are, back row, left to right – Joe Petrilla (tail gunner), Leon Metzler (waist gunner), Phil Rosenberg (radio operator), Ted Stienle (ball turret gunner) and Tony Lanzano (flight engineer). Front row, left to right – Eugene Arnold Jr (pilot), Frank Corrado (bombardier), Ron Fowler (co-pilot) and Joe Butkiewicz (navigator) (*Eugene Arnold Jr*)

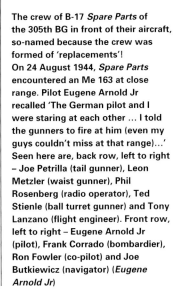

These photographs taken from the camera gun fitted to Feldwebel Siegfried Schubert's Me 163 were shown to the *Oberkommando der Luftwaffe* and led to the *General der Jagdflieger*, Adolf Galland, issuing a memorandum on 8 September 1944 declaring the Me 163 fully operational. Note that the damage inflicted on Lavadiere's B-17 is similar to that shown in these photographs (*JG 400 Archive*)

B-17 (WF-P, *Spare Parts*, 2nd Lt E Arnold Jr), 305th BG, attacked.
B-17 (WF-S, 2nd Lt H K Wetherhold), 305th BG, attacked.
B-17 (42-97571, Lt Winfred Pugh), 457th BG, shot down, claimed by Feldwebel Siegfried Schubert.

Leutnant Bott later recalled;

'On 24 August 1944 there were eight Me 163s available for seven operational pilots. My first combat sortie should have taken place a few days earlier but on that occasion I had experienced my first engine flame out. My *Staffel* [1./JG 400] climbed to a high altitude and we suddenly saw below us to port a formation of B-17 bombers flying at a height of about 9,000 metres. I dived without power – I had already shut down the engine on levelling out – in order to get behind the bombers but, after completing the dive, I was relieved to find that I could no longer see them. I landed but then felt an unaccountable rage well up. On landing I saw the eighth aircraft and told my driver to take me to it. I recognised the aircraft as one that I had flown previously, because it was the only one armed with two MG 151 machine guns [probably White 2].

'I used almost the whole length of the runway to take off, the combustion chamber pressure being too low at 22 atmospheres. The course I had to fly took me towards Leipzig. I encountered a formation of bombers while still climbing and fired at an aircraft on the port side of the formation. As soon as I began firing my MG 151 machine guns one of them jammed but the other continued to fire and I saw my shells hit the aircraft. Using the last of my fuel, I carried on climbing to 9,000 metres and dived back down at high speed. I was in the air for seven minutes.'

A Flak battery later confirmed that the aircraft he had attacked had crashed and he was awarded the EK II.

After this attack 1./JG 400 submitted the following report to the OKL;

'On 24 August 1944, eight Me 163s took off for a mission against enemy bomber formations. The take-off comprised three pairs of aircraft and two single aircraft. Three aircraft made contact with the enemy, three sighted the aircraft and two did not sight the enemy. The first pair only sighted the enemy shortly before landing.

'The second pair climbed to 10,000-11,000 metres. With their engines switched off, both aircraft glided to 6,000 metres before sighting an enemy bomber formation which was flying at 6,500 metres. Feldwebel [Siegfried] Schubert, the leader of the pair, immediately started his engine and attacked the formation leader, achieving hits in the port wing. In a second attack on another four-engined aircraft hits were achieved in the starboard wing. The bomber fell away in a dive, burning and afterwards turning over its right wing into a spin. Victory!

'The engine of the second Me 163 of the pair cut out a few seconds after re-starting, and an attempt to get the motor going again was unsuccessful. The fuel supply was exhausted and the flight was broken off.

'The third pair sighted the enemy at 3,000 metres. The first attack was a frontal one, but the ingress of fuel fumes in the cockpit hindered vision. In attempting to attack the formation from above the fuel supply was exhausted. Effective firing was therefore no longer possible.

'The next take-off of a single aircraft was doomed to failure, it being abandoned at 3,000 metres.

'The single aircraft taking off last had full sight of the enemy from the beginning and made contact at a height of 7,000 metres. The pilot, Leutnant Bott, carried out two approaches using low thrust and scored hits in the port wing. After attacking the enemy aircraft his engine cut out. Without thrust a third attack was carried out. Hits could no longer be observed. Three crew members were observed to bale out.

'The first *Staffel* has thus achieved the first five successes with the Me 163.

At the beginning of September 1944, Hauptmann Otto Böhner transferred with his squadron to Brandis. In April 1945, he was ordered to join the German Army at Eger (Cheb), Czechoslovakia (*JG 400 Archive*)

'It was thus proved that the Me 163 could not only intercept and destroy single aircraft, as was previously assumed, but can also effectively attack bomber formations. The five aircraft which took off on 16 August 1944 achieved two kills. The eight aircraft on 24 August 1944 achieved three kills. It had been possible to score two kills in one flight.

'Particularly significant is the experience that the occurrence of inadequate sealing of the powerplant or engine leads to an intense accumulation of vapour in the cockpit. Deficient vision through misting of the cockpit canopy and tears almost inevitably leads to breaking off the flight.

'The operational flights revealed that the engine often cuts out at high altitude due to fuel starvation, this probably being due to negative acceleration in the transition from climb to horizontal flight. Immediate attempts at starting were successful. Time must be allowed for ventilating the engine's turbo-pump. This has again revealed the urgency of testing the new tank equipment.'

Unteroffizier Kurt Schiebeler in Me 163B White 1, who took off at 1200 hrs and landed at 1215 hrs, and Feldwebel Rudolf Zimmermann, Me 163B White 3, were also involved in these attacks.

On 6 September 1944, 2./JG 400 under the command of Hauptmann Otto Böhner arrived at Brandis.

Two days later, Major Wolfgang Späte was officially appointed *Gruppenkommandeur* I./JG 400 but was unable to take up his post immediately. On the same day, the *General der Jagdflieger* Adolf Galland declared the Me 163 operational;

'The first operational *Staffel* has shot down three four-engined bombers with certainty and two probably and has confirmed the usefulness of and the tactics envisaged for this aircraft in combat. Measures will be taken to increase the number of each squadron's aircraft and pilots to 20 in order to improve their effectiveness. The aircraft's readiness has been up till now adversely impaired by the lack of spare parts for the airframe and engine. The aircraft can now be declared to be operationally ready.'

Reinhard Opitz, who was later to become *Staffelkapitän* of 7./JG 400, recalled that on 9 September there was an unusual event, which he still remembers well;

'Prof. Ritter, the son of the well-known Ufa film director and an Oberleutnant serving with a Propaganda Company, was contracted to produce a film about the Me 163. I flew Ritter and his two cameramen on alternate occasions in the Bf 110. In order to allow enough room for the cameramen to operate their cameras, the rear part of the cockpit canopy normally occupied by twin machine-guns was removed. We flew many times to several thousand metres with an Me 163 in tow and the cameramen in the rear of the Bf 110. After the tow-line had been released, I descended to 2,000 metres so that the Me 163 could be filmed making a mock attack on our aircraft. We performed fly-pasts, stalls, and climbs while turning to port and starboard to complete the film sequences, and a preview of the film showed that the result would be useful for the purpose for which it was intended.

'It has to be remembered that sharp take-offs were then still a rarity. On the day planned for filming such an event – clouds in the background were a pre-requisite for the film – Ritter positioned his cameramen at the start, in the middle and at the end of the runway. I had just completed a series of towed take-offs with the Bf 110 and had jettisoned the towline and was about to land on the grass landing strip when I saw a Me 163 begin its take-off from the concrete runway in front of me. On landing in the Bf 110, I noticed the Me 163 had reached the end of the runway and then I saw it climb unusually steeply. Smoke streaming below the fuselage indicated that the aircraft was in trouble; it appeared as though the motor had cut out soon after the aircraft had taken off. The aircraft stalled at a height of about 100-150 metres. In the same instant the canopy was jettisoned and the pilot baled out. I didn't notice the parachute open because from the same direction a cloud of smoke billowed up from the explosion as the Me 163 hit the ground. Kelb was the name of the pilot who managed to find a gravel pit on the northeast side of the airfield that was just as deep as the height needed to deploy the parachute and brake his fall.

'Ritter and his crew had filmed everything from beginning to end and, with a good deal of laughter, we watched the film strip a few days later in the *Fliegerhorst*'s mess.'

Rolf Glogner added;

'Oberfeldwebel Husser and I were each to fly an Me 163B to test the aircraft after maintenance. Kelb took off first and his engine cut out at a height of 80 metres. He climbed, turned to port and baled out. The event was filmed by Ritter. Böhner asked us if we still wished to fly to which we naturally replied that we did. We started our engines and just at that moment, a car trailing a cloud of dust raced across the airfield towards us. A mechanic climbed out and called on us to stop. Both aircraft were taken back to the hangar to have their engines checked. The mechanics found splits in the fuel lines of both aircraft caused by a material defect. I celebrated my "birthday" in the evening.'

On 11 September 1944, the Eighth Air Force mounted bombing raids on Ruhland, Böhlen, Brüx and Chemnitz, ten combat wings totalling 384 B-17 Fortresses taking part in the attacks. The bombers were escorted by 275 P-51 Mustangs. The weather conditions over the target areas were cloudy. The attack began from an intercept point about 40km south of Merseburg at 1149 hrs. Ruhland, Brüx and Chemnitz were attacked at 1223 hrs from 24,500 to 27,000 feet. Böhlen was attacked at about 1215 hrs. After the attacks the bombers reassembled at a point well west of the target areas at 1359 hrs.

Most of the ten bombers from the attack on Ruhland followed the planned flight path south of Brandis, the flight to Ruhland being further south than the return route. The exception was a lone straggler heading for Ruhland from Group 486 C, 3rd Bombardment Division, which flew to the north and too close to the airfield at Brandis. Unteroffizier Kurt Schiebeler of 1./JG 400 was scrambled to attack. He later recalled;

'After my second sharp take-off, Oberleutnant Franz Rösle asked me, even though I had also made two sharp take-offs that day, to fly the third sortie for him. I took off in "White 2". There were bombers heading towards Dresden and a lone B-17 flew over the airfield. I flew towards the bomber too quickly and my shots went wide. I made a gliding second attack but again did not score any hits on the aircraft. During my third gliding attack, my shells hit the starboard, inboard

Leutnant Friedrich 'Fritz' Kelb, 2./JG 400, joined Major Wolfgang Späte at JG 7, Prague-Ruzyne, in April 1945. He was shot down and killed in an Me 262 on 30 April 1945 (*JG 400 Archive*)

Unteroffizier Kurt Schiebeler, 1./JG 400, served with JG 54 in Russia before he joined EKdo 16 and JG 400. He claimed a total of six victories, five of them in Russia. He was awarded the *Frontflug-Spange* in Silver for fighter pilots on 21 September and the EK II in the field on 10 October 1944. Schiebeler was later promoted to Feldwebel while serving with JG 400. On 13 April 1945, Schiebeler and his wingman, Hans Wiedemann, took off to join Major Späte at Prague-Ruzyne but the flight had to be discontinued because they were attacked by three Thunderbolts. Wiedemann was shot down over Döbeln and killed. Schiebeler returned to Brandis and took off again for Prague in a Bf 110, landing there 35 minutes later (*JG 400 Archive*)

bomber's crew were picked up and brought to the airfield, where they met Schiebeler. Schiebeler was airborne between 1236 and 1250 hrs. As the Me 163B flown in the attack was armed with MG 151 machine guns it was probably one of the aircraft originally delivered by Hanns Klemm Flugzeugbau GmbH from Böblingen to Wittmundhafen and transferred with 1./JG 400 to Brandis in July 1944.

The accident in which Oberleutnant Franz Rösle, 1./JG 400, sustained severe facial injuries is believed to have taken place on 13 September. Rösle himself cannot recall the exact date but it is known that it took place before 28 September when he sustained even more serious injuries. In a letter to Mano Ziegler, he wrote;

'I had been scrambled to intercept enemy bombers. Unfortunately, as was often the case, the engine cut out during take-off. At 600 metres, I pulled the fuel dump handle in order to get rid of all my *C-Stoff* and *T-Stoff* as quickly as possible before turning to make a landing. Everything went according to plan. I landed with the skid extended, sped over the grass and then it happened – the damned thing exploded! The pain in my face was driving me mad and I had only one thought in mind: I had to get away from the crate as the whole aircraft could have blown up at any moment. Luckily, the fire brigade arrived quickly and I yelled for water. My face was promptly doused by a jet of water and I then felt only a burning sensation.

'There was only one officer on the airfield itself and he took care of me, the rest having moved to the command post located outside the airfield in order to control combat operations. Unfortunately, our doctor

Two views of Me 163B 'White 14', showing it marked with slightly different forms of squadron code number and camouflage. The overall camouflage scheme suggests that the aircraft was built by Klemm. Apart from the fact that the aircraft was filmed as it was towed across the airfield nothing is known of its history (*JG 400 Archive*)

and ambulance had also been evacuated to safety. I was taken to the cellar below the control tower from where a doctor was to be called by telephone. As I entered the cellar, both of the female telephone operators ran screaming from the room – I must have been a beautiful sight. This situation delayed the arrival of the ambulance by about 20 minutes and I wouldn't like to have to go through that time ever again. After treatment in hospital, I spent three months wearing a mask over my face. It is likely that the explosion was caused by some of the *T-Stoff* collecting in the skid after I had jettisoned the fuel and then catching fire from the heat generated by friction between the skid and the ground as I slid over the airfield after touching down. This was the second blow and the third was soon to follow [on 28 September].'

Rolf Glogner also recalled this accident;

'Rösle pulled the fuel emergency jettison handle after the engine had cut out on take-off and some of the fuel collected in the skid's fairing. The heat generated in the skid during landing set fire to the fuel and a flame shot through the cockpit. Afterwards, Rösle had to eat his meals in front of a mirror because his head was so heavily bandaged.'

On 28 September 1944, the Eighth Air Force bombed the oil refineries at Merseburg-Leuna. The report on the attack recorded;

'Two ineffectual passes by two Me 163s were made on B-17s of [the] 2nd Force in the target area at 1157-1210 hrs [301 B-17s attacked the refineries] and the '2nd Force fighter escort encountered several scattered Me 163s over the target area about 1200 hrs. One pilot claimed one Me 163 as probably destroyed in the target area at 1210 hrs.'

The encounter report made by 1st Lt Edward L Wilsey, 374th FS, 361st FG, reads;

Me 163s at the eastern end of the runway. Grass from the airfield was cut and stacked along the airfield's perimeter, one eyewitness maintaining that the stacks were used to catch the Me 163s undercarriage dollies after they had been jettisoned and bounced across the airfield. The large aircraft in the background is the first prototype of the Junkers Ju 287 forward swept-winged bomber (*EN Archive*)

Oberleutnant Franz Rösle served with 1./JG 400 at Wittmundhafen and Brandis from March 1944 to April 1945. In September, he not only sustained severe facial injuries during a landing accident when his aircraft caught fire but also injured a vertebra in the lumbar region after baling out of his Me 163 at very low altitude. He was given the rank of *Staffelführer* on the formation of 3./JG 400 at Brandis in November 1944 (*JG 400 Archive*)

Me 163 'White 11'. Its externally visible features indicate that it might have come from the same batch of aircraft as 'White 10', which was built by Junkers. This photograph was taken on 15 November 1944 (*Uwe Frömert with permission*)

'I was flying on left side of bombers, slightly below, at Merseberg [*sic*, Merseburg], 1210 hrs when I saw what I believed to be a large rocket come up out of target area. Immediately afterwards I saw the contrail stop and the aeroplane appeared, which made a pass through bombers from rear to front going up, then made 180-degree wingover and dove back through bombers doing an aileron roll to right and continued dive, passing within 400 yards of me. I picked him up in K-14 sight and gave him a squirt. He flicked to the right and back again and then dove down to the left. I dove after him picking him up in K-14 sight [*sic*] at short intervals giving him a squirt each time as he was pulling away from me. My aeroplane started shuddering and vibrating badly. I checked my airspeed and it was over 500mph. I pulled out to the right when at 8,000 feet at which time the Me 163 was going straight down definitely pulling away from me, and I did not see him again.

'Observations: This Me 163 had terrific speed and excellent aileron control. Highly manoeuvrable at all speeds. High rate of speed in climb of 75 to 80 degrees. Power appeared to be used only on climbing or straight level flight, with no reduction in speed when power shut off. Appeared to be painted black. No features of armament were observed. Wingman Flt Off Voss saw Me 163 still heading straight down at approximately 5,000 feet as he (Voss) pulled out at 7,000 feet, and did not see jet after pull out. I claim this Me 163 probably destroyed.'

Feldwebel Rudolf Zimmermann flew an operational sortie that day in Me 163B V62 (Wk-Nr. 16310071 'White 7').

Oberleutnant Franz Rösle was once more badly injured in an accident on 28 September;

'I took off and once again the engine flamed out, this time, however, at the dangerous height of 300-400 metres. I turned back to the airfield and pulled the handle to jettison the fuel. I recognised the danger in delay and the need to react quickly but there was no time left to make a normal landing. There was an explosion and my head became alarmingly hot. I had to bale out. My altitude was just 250 metres. I released my seat

harness and pulled the canopy emergency jettison handle. Nothing happened. The tension mounted. What could I do? I attempted to push the canopy upwards with both hands and it unexpectedly fell to one side but did not fly away. At least my escape route was free. I let myself fall out sideways and rearwards.

'At that moment the Me 163 rolled, the canopy fell shut and I was left hanging outside the aircraft with my feet clamped between the canopy and the cockpit sill and my body hanging along the side of the fuselage. Fortunately, I was wearing my fur-lined flying boots and I was able to pull a foot out of one of them, and with the freed foot push myself away from the aircraft. According to eye-witnesses, I baled out at a height of not more than 100-120 metres. I immediately pulled the parachute's rip cord and felt the shock as the parachute opened and only then realised that I was falling far too quickly. I hit the ground and blacked out.

'As I came round in hospital I saw some familiar faces above me, including that of the doctor. From their expression, I realised that there was something wrong with me. X-rays taken at the hospital showed that I had injured a vertebra in the lumbar region. I spent the next nine months encased in a plaster corset.'

The *Namentliche Verlustmeldung* states that Oberleutnant Rösle suffered his injuries after a combat sortie on 28 September 1944, when he was flying Me 163B V49 Wk-Nr. 16310058 PK+QT. The aircraft was 60% damaged. Rösle states that his face remained bandaged for three months after his previous accident and, therefore, he must have flown his sortie on 28 September with his face bandaged, which might account for his comment that 'his head became alarmingly hot'.

A frame taken from a training film showing 'White 14' being towed to the runway at Brandis. 'White 11' can be seen inside the hangar, the Me 163 bearing a distinctive light green camouflage patch on its fin (*JG 400 Archive*)

According to official documents, 3./JG 400 was in the process of being formed in August 1944 and was to be based at Stargard. In November, the squadron was renumbered 5./JG 400 and a new squadron with the original designation 3./JG 400 was formed at Brandis. The renumbering of the squadrons has led to considerable confusion, especially since various sources state that Rösle was the designated *Staffelführer* of 3./JG 400. The authors believe that Rösle was entrusted with the establishment of 3./JG 400 in August 1944 and designated to lead the squadron at Stargard. His accident on 28 September put paid to him becoming *Staffelführer* of 5./JG 400 and he was replaced by Leutnant Peter Gerth. After his accident, Rösle also stated that he spent the next nine months, i.e. until June 1945, in a plaster corset, but according to Luftwaffe personnel records he was made *Staffelkapitän* of 3./JG 400 in February 1945. It is possible that the Luftwaffe's records are incorrect, or that Rösle was, in fact, given command of the 'new' 3./JG 400, although how he could have accomplished this task, in view of his injuries, is not clear.

Erprobungskommando 16 arrived at Brandis during the evening of 8 October. Three Bf 110s and two Me 163s were flown to Brandis, the latter under tow. On arrival at Brandis, EKdo 16 discovered there were no workshops and no storerooms it could use because, as it had noted in its report for September, Brandis was overcrowded. A protest from Hauptmann Thaler resulted in the transfer of *Ergänzungsstaffel*/JG 400 to Udetfeld in Upper Silesia, the unit being stationed there after 15 October. EKdo 16 was then able to take over some workshops and quarters and to begin conducting makeshift repairs to the aircraft. However, the hangar allotted to EKdo 16 had been so badly damaged by a bomb dropped during the 28 May attack on the airfield that it could not be heated and its doors could not be closed. Another protest to Oberst

Another frame from the training film showing the recovery of an Me 163 after landing with the Scheuch-Schlepper, a form of fork-lift trailer (*JG 400 Archive*)

JG 400 was visited by Oberst Gordon Gollob, *Typenbegleiter* Me 163, in late September or early October 1944. He was escorted by Oberleutnant Ernst Siebert, Hauptmann Bernhard Graf von Schweinitz and Herr Sachse, an engineer seconded to the *Rüstungsministerium*, where he was responsible for the mass production of the Me 163B. (Sachse had previously been engaged in the production of the Tiger tank.) Gollob flew both the Me 163A and B during this visit. He later succeeded Adolf Galland as *General der Jagdflieger* (*JG 400 Archive*)

Gollob resulted in Junkers' engine flight test department and EKdo 16 changing places with one another, and the *Erprobungskommando* sharing a heated hangar with Junkers' aircraft flight test department, which allowed them to work closely together. The seven aircraft then at EKdo 16's disposal were BV30 (C1+02), BV40 (C1+03), BV45 (C1+05), BV?? (C1+08), Klemm-built Me 163B-0 Wk-Nr. 440008 (C1+11), BV14 (C1+12) and BV35 (C1+13).

In the meantime, KdE's proposal to reduce the *Erprobungskommando*'s size had been discussed and it was agreed that the overall strength of EKdo 16 would be 147, including officers, officials, non-commissioned

Rocket engines were sometimes tested inside the entrance to the hangar. Note the *T-Stoff* and *C-Stoff* refuelling funnels are still in position. On one occasion this practice led to an explosion in which personnel were injured and the hangar roof was damaged (*JG 400 Archive*)

*Ergänzungsstaffel/*JG 400, autumn 1944. This photograph was taken at Brandis after Herbert Hentschel cartwheeled with an Me 163B during a landing outside Brandis airfield. Standing, left to right, unknown, Udo Schwenger, Herbert Hentschel, Anton Süss and Werner Husemann (*JG 400 Archive*)

Right
Hauptmann Robert Olejnik commanded 1./JG 400 until December 1944, when he became *Gruppenkommandeur* **of IV./EJG 2, based at Sprottau, and at the end of January 1945, transferred with IV.** *Gruppe* **to Esperstedt where it remained till mid-April. Olejnik returned to Brandis shortly before the evacuation of the airfield in April and joined an army unit ordered to move south through Dresden to Eger (Cheb), Czechoslovakia, where he was taken prisoner by American forces. He ended the war credited with 42 victories (***JG 400 Archive***)**

Far right
Unteroffizier Werner Husemann was born in Essen on 13 March 1922 and died in Berlin on 11 August 1990. He was promoted to Unteroffizier with effect from 1 December 1943. At the end of the war he was held as a PoW by the Americans at Zwickau, but managed to escape with his comrade Feldwebel Ernst Schelper, who served with 2./JG 400 (*JG 400 Archive***)**

officers and other ranks. Its surplus personnel were to be used to establish the fourth *Staffel* of I./JG 400 and to reinforce *Ergänzungsstaffel/*JG 400.

The *Ergänzungsstaffel/*JG 400 was renamed the 13th *Staffel* on the creation of the fourth *Gruppe* of *Ergänzungsjagdgeschwader* 2, and together with 14./EJG 2 they were responsible for Me 163 pilot training. Both units were probably formed after 1 November 1944. The 13th *Staffel* was stationed at the Luftwaffe's test centre at Udetfeld (Zendek, Poland) and 14./EJG 2 at the airfield at Sprottau (Szprotawa, Poland). There is the possibility that another *Staffel*, 15./EJG 2, was formed under the command of Hauptmann Erwin Sturm.

From December 1944 onwards Hauptmann Robert Olejnik was in command of IV./EJG 2. The *Geschwaderstab/*EJG 2 was also at Sprottau for part of the time.

Oberleutnant Adolf Niemeyer was *Staffelführer* of 13./EJG 2 for the period November 1944 to March 1945. Unteroffizier Werner Husemann wrote of the training in Udetfeld: 'We also practised aerial gunnery with the *Stummel-Habicht* glider with Helmut Reukauf as instructor. We made the first flights with an aircraft with a gunsight and there were also two *Stummel-Habicht* both armed with a machine pistol, but this initial training wasn't continued. In the meantime Charly Magersuppe [Carl Marsen] made a very good aerobatic flight with the *Habicht*.' 13./EJG 2 transferred from Udetfeld to Esperstedt, arriving on 29 January 1945.

The 14th *Staffel*, under the command of Leutnant Hermann 'Mano' Ziegler, set itself up at the airfield at Sprottau and called its living quarters '*Klein Zieglersdorf*' in honour of its *Staffelkapitän*. 14./EJG 2 was forced to leave the airfield at Sprottau in January 1945 because the Soviet Army was approaching. The squadron was transferred by various routes to the airfield at Esperstedt in Thüringen.

According to Robert Olejnik, the *Geschwaderstab* of EJG 2 transferred to Schleswig-Holstein three weeks later (that is, after 28 February 1945) and the remaining personnel were sent to fight with the army near

Esperstedt and Schafstädt. He himself drove with the vehicles of IV./EJG 2 to Brandis on 25 March 1945. Oberleutnant Niemeyer and his *Staffel*, 13./EJG 2, was put under the command of General Schörner's division and sent to take part in the fighting in Czechoslovakia from the middle of March.

On 7 October 1944, the Eighth Air Force bombed Böhlen, Lützkendorf, Merseburg, Leuna, Wurzen and Rositz. The USAAF reported;

'Approximately 40-50 enemy aircraft attacked [3rd Force combat wings despatched to attack Böhlen] in the area southwest of Leipzig from 1201-1209 hrs. Enemy aircraft were mostly Fw 190s with a few Me 109s, Me 410s and two Me 163s. They made a mass attack out of the clouds from the rear high to level in waves of eight to ten abreast peeling off to right, left, and some going under formation. Pilots were very aggressive except for Me 163s of which the pilots seem inexperienced. Attack lasted for approximately eight minutes and although supporting fighters were in the immediate area and attacked the enemy aircraft they were unable to prevent a loss of 12 B-17s to the saturation attack.' [86 B-17s attacked the synthetic oil refinery at Böhlen.]

'2nd Force B-17s despatched against Ruhland reported one attack by four Me 163s on a straggler five miles northwest of Chemnitz. Attacks were made at 1225 hrs from 19,000 feet and only one pass was made before supporting P-51s came in to chase the enemy aircraft. Bomber crews reported that speed of the Me 163 seemed no greater than that of P-51s during the attack.

'One Me 163 attacked a B-17 box east of Leipzig at 1231 hrs and another attacked again at 1235 hrs. The enemy aircraft were chased by supporting fighters in each case.'

Ethell's research revealed that the following USAAF aircraft were attacked during this bombing raid;

B-17 (ET-B, 2nd Lt R M Brown), 95th BG, attacked by Feldwebel Siegfried Schubert.

B-17 (ET-Q, 2nd Lt W Hart), 95th BG, attacked by Oberfeldwebel Fritz Husser.

B-17 (QW-E, 2nd Lt M A Hendrickson), 95th BG, attacked.

B-17 (QW-F, 1st Lt R S Lash), 95th BG, attacked.

B-17 (QW-T, 2nd Lt H C Coffman), 95th BG, attacked.

B-17 (QW-Y, 2nd Lt B B Busse), 95th BG, attacked.

B-17 (42-102560, 1st Lt N F Day), 95th BG, attacked by Leutnant Bott and claimed by him destroyed.

B-17 95th BG, attacked and shot down by Feldwebel Schubert. Attack witnessed by pilots of 352nd FG. Six crew members baled out.

B-17 (2nd Lt P E Ristine), 95th BG, attacked.

B-17 (*Los Angeles City Limits*, 1st Lt John T O'Conner), 381st BG, attacked.

According to Oberfeldwebel Friedrich-Peter 'Fritz' Husser;

'Feldwebel Siegfried Schubert and Leutnant Hans Bott were the first to take off – Schubert was about 50 metres ahead of Bott. Suddenly, flames

Hermann 'Mano' Ziegler enlisted in the Luftwaffe at the outbreak of war, rising to rank of Leutnant. He volunteered for service with EKdo 16, joining that unit at Bad Zwischenahn in October 1943. Ziegler was seconded to Jesau as technical officer in June to assist with flight testing Me 163s completed by Klemm, returning to Bad Zwischenahn in July 1944. He transferred to *Ergänzungsstaffel/ JG 400* at Brandis in September and two months later was promoted to *Staffelführer/Staffelkapitän* of 14./EJG 2, with which he served at Rangsdorf, Sprottau and Esperstedt before returning to Brandis in February 1945 (*JG 400 Archive*)

Oberfeldwebel 'Fritz' Husser, who served with both 1. and 2./JG 400, survived this crash landing after overshooting the airfield on his return to Brandis from an unsuccessful combat sortie on 7 October. On this occasion Husser was flying Klemm-built Me 163B Wk-Nr. 440165 (*EN Archive*)

shot out from Schubert's Me 163: the rocket's combustion chamber had caught fire. His speed was then about 60km/h. The aircraft rolled onto the grass and somersaulted because of the position of its centre-of-gravity which was high (his aircraft was fully fuelled). [Feldwebel Schubert, 1./JG 400, was flying Me 163B V61 Wk-Nr. 16310070 GN+MD. Some sources say that this was the second take-off he had made that day.]

'Unteroffizier Manfred Eisenmann and I were ordered to take off next but we made no contact with the enemy as it had by then completed its attack and the next formation of bombers could not be seen. These appeared, however, just after we had begun to make our approach to land and it looked as though the bombers were going to attack the airfield. In the meantime, the wind direction had changed and a tail-wind was blowing, giving me the feeling that my landing flaps were not operating properly.

Lt Ralph M Brown and the usual crew of his 95th BG B-17 which was attacked by Feldwebel Siegfried Schubert of 1./JG 400 on 7 October 1944, with the exception that Brown's usual co-pilot (Evans) is shown rather than the substitute Philpott who actually flew on 7 October (Evans was wounded at the time). These men are, front row, Waters (bombardier), Hadlock (navigator), Brown (pilot), Evans (co-pilot), Urankar (radar navigator for lead crew). Back row, Malloy (ball turret gunner), Kametler (waist gunner), Shue (engineer), Howard (radio operator) (*L R Brown*)

'My main desire was to land as quickly as possible before the bombs began to rain down and in doing so I made a heavy landing. My aircraft bounced 200 metres into the air and then glided over the perimeter fence, eventually landing in a sand pit where the Me 163 flipped over onto its back. A soldier called to me, "Get out, it's going to explode!" I, with blood streaming over my face, could not move. Behind me I could hear the rocket motor still rumbling. I was eventually rescued by Unteroffizier Harald Kuhn from HWK, who smashed the plexiglass canopy and pulled me out of the cockpit. [Husser was flying Klemm-built Me 163B Wk-Nr. 440165 the aircraft was 65% damaged.]

'Eisenmann also began his approach to land from too great a height. He slammed down hard on the ground and was catapulted back up into the air. The aircraft performed a number of rolls and then a cartwheel as one of its wingtips hit the ground. The aircraft was completely destroyed. Eisenmann was thrown out of the cockpit and died from his injuries (fractured skull).'

Eisenmann, an only son, was flying Klemm-built Me 163B Wk-Nr. 440013 BQ+UP when this fatal accident took place.

Unteroffizier Rolf Glogner;

'Feldwebel Schubert took off with a tailwind (the wind had turned suddenly) to intercept a formation of B-17s. Halfway along the runway, the engine in Schubert's aircraft cut out and he rolled onto the grass to get out of the way of the other aircraft which were following him. One of his wings touched the ground and his aircraft somersaulted and then exploded just as the aircraft flown by Bott passed him. I was in the last aircraft and was waiting for clearance to take off. Aircraft then began returning from their sorties approaching the runway against the wind and heading directly towards me! Oberfeldwebel Husser was flying too fast and flew over the perimeter fence and through a hedge and then landed in a meadow, his aircraft turning over onto its back.

'Despite the risk to themselves from an explosion, the groundcrew pulled Husser out of the cockpit. He sustained a dislocated arm, a broken nose and concussion. Then Eisenmann arrived, too high and too fast. He sideslipped and the wing of his aircraft hit the ground. The aircraft disintegrated and Eisenmann was thrown out still harnessed to his seat, hitting the ground 100 metres in front of me. He was dead. Feldwebel Straznicky was also killed in combat that day.

'In the meantime, a smoke signal from a Very pistol had been fired to indicate that a bomber formation was approaching the airfield. I clambered out of my aircraft and stumbled like a drunk in full flying kit over to a trench to take cover. The bombers headed towards Leipzig and the all clear was given and I stumbled back to my aircraft. I was then given clearance to take off and passed two dead comrades as I gained speed along the runway. Don't ask me what my feelings were, especially as I was unable to catch up with the enemy because the ground controllers had already shut down the radar – the idiots.'

Unteroffizier Kurt Schiebeler, who was flying Me 163B 'White 3', claimed the *Herausschuss* of the lead aircraft of the formation of ten B-17s. He took off at 1230 hrs and landed nine minutes later.

At 1230 hrs. Lieutenants Elmer A Taylor and Willard G Erfkamp, flying P-51 Mustangs of the 385th FS, 364th FG, were in the vicinity of Leipzig. Taylor reported;

'I was leading Yellow Section at 25,000 feet, escorting bombers around the target when I observed a jet making passes at a straggling B-17. I made a wide turn to come in on him from his rear. I was about 2,000 feet higher than he was, so I soon closed on him. I started shooting at 1,500 yards hoping to damage him and keep him from renewing his attack on the bomber. Evidently, he had his power out as I closed quite rapidly at 2,400 rpm with 30 inches of mercury. I still had both belly tanks on because I didn't think I had a chance of catching it. I closed quite rapidly to 100 yards, chopped my throttle to stay behind and opened fire. I observed many strikes on the tail, fuselage, and both wings. The jet rolled over and dived straight down, emitting a trail of white smoke. My element followed it down, staying with it at approx 500mph. The jet bellied in a field, and my element strafed it, causing it to explode and burn. The pilot did not get out of the ship. I claim one (1) Me 163 destroyed and shared with Lt Erfkamp.'

Lt Willard G. Erfkamp recorded;

'I was flying No 3 position in Yellow Section escorting bombers around the target at 25,000 feet. We sighted an Me 163 making passes at a straggling B-17. Lt Taylor, leader of Yellow Section led us in a wide turn which took us down to 23,000 feet and brought us in behind the jet. Lt Taylor fired scoring many hits on him and then seeing that he was going to over-shoot the jet told us to follow the jet. My wingman and I chased the jet all the way to the ground, indicating 500mph, firing and observing some strikes as we were plummeting down. He landed on a grass field and started to climb out. We made a pass strafing him. He fell back into the cockpit and we did a wing-over and strafed the ship from the opposite direction. The nose blew up and the ship burned. I claim one (1) Me 163 destroyed and shared with Lt Taylor.'

On this occasion, the 65th Fighter Wing reported;

'Combat with Me 163 ensued north of target at 1230 hrs, 17,000 feet. Jet aeroplane seen attacking straggler. Enemy aircraft at 20,000

American pilots of 65th Fighter Wing who attacked the Me 163 flown by Feldwebel Rudolf Zimmermann. From left to right, Lt Elmer A Taylor, Lt Willard G Erfkamp and Lt Everett N Farrell (*USAF*)

feet was attacked from 25,000 feet by Lt Taylor of 385th FS [364th FG]. Attack on enemy aircraft made from rear, closing from 1,500 to 150 yards with many strikes observed on wings and fuselage. Enemy aircraft apparently taken by surprise. Me 163 then went into steep spiralling dive at approximately 500mph and was followed by Lt Erfkamp and [Everett N] Farrell. The Me 163 then belly landed into a field apparently under perfect control. Lts Erfkamp and Farrell then strafed enemy aircraft setting it on fire and believed to have killed the pilot who was caught in the field of fire.'

In fact, Zimmermann survived this attack. He had managed to jump out of the cockpit and ran off as the Mustangs began strafing his aircraft. He flew Me 163B V62 Wk-Nr. 16310071 'White 7' that day and landed at Borna after the sortie. Schiebeler made a test flight in 'White 7' on 22 November 1944.

On 14 October 1944, Hauptmann Rudolf Opitz was ordered to take over temporary command of I./JG 400 for four weeks while Späte recovered from illness.

The fiercest fighting and the last major engagement involving Me 163s from I./JG 400 took place on 2 November 1944, when the Eighth Air Force again bombed the Merseburg-Leuna refineries.

The USAAF Intops Summary reported;

'Approximately nine Me 163s made single attacks on one group of 1st Force. Group 1 of 1st Force fighter escort encountered 15+ Me 163s and 4+ Me 109s south and east of Merseburg. Two Me 163s and two Me 109s claimed destroyed in combat with fighter escort: one of Me 163s passed through bomber formation in target area and was caught by fighter group leader while making 180-degree turn; other Me 163 destroyed in similar manner near Leipzig. Group 6 saw two jet-propelled aircraft north of Zeitz and in vicinity of Einbeck [near Bad Gandersheim, probably Me 262]. Group 7 of 1st Force fighter escort encountered four jet-propelled aircraft before target [possibly Merseburg] but enemy aircraft evaded. Group 8 of 1st Force fighter escort saw six Me 163s in vicinity of Naumburg, evading due to high speed.

'2nd Force was attacked by Me 109s, Fw 190s and a few Me 163s.'

On 7 October 1944, after an attack on a B-17 of the 95th BG, Feldwebel Rudolf Zimmermann, 1./JG 400, was pursued by Lieutenants Taylor, Erfkamp and Farrell from the 364th FG. Although his aircraft was hit, Zimmermann escaped the attempts to shoot him down and survived the strafing attacks, despite the claims made by Erfkamp and Farrell, after making a forced landing near Borna. Zimmermann was flying Me 163B V62 'White 7' that day. Feldwebel Zimmermann began his flying career in 1937 when he was 15 years old. Between 1940 and May 1943 he received training at Königsberg, with the *Fliegerausbildungsregiment* (FAR) 21 at Deblin in Poland, FAR 41 at Eggersdorf, the Fighter School at Werneuchen and the Fighter Pilots School at La Rochelle in France. In this period he made some 609 flights with various types of aircraft. In May 1943, he was posted to 10./JG 27 at Kalamaki, Greece, where he made 60 flights but never saw combat. He underwent glider training at Gelnhausen in September 1943 and was posted to EKdo 16 that same month. He transferred to 1./JG 400 at Wittmundhafen in May 1944 and moved with that squadron to Brandis the following July (*JG 400 Archive*)

The 65th Fighter Wing recorded;

'Approximately 15 Me 163s were encountered by the 4th FG on today's mission (Merseburg) while screening the target area on the east side. The enemy aircraft came up singly and in a 45/60-degree climb emitting black and white smoke trails. The smoke trails cut off at bomber altitude.

'One Me 163 climbed through the flak and the bomber formation at target, cut off his jet and made a 180-degree turn, heading east. Captain Fred N Glover, 336th FS, slid in unobserved, behind the enemy aircraft as it turned and fired a two second burst from 400 yards, getting strikes immediately on the Me 163. The belly of the aircraft exploded and flame enveloped the fuselage. The enemy aircraft wallowed down like a falling leaf and at 8,000 feet the pilot baled out.

'A second Me 163 was attacked by Captain Louis N Norley, 335th FS, five minutes later south of Leipzig. Orbiting beneath the overcast (25,000 feet) Captain Norley observed the enemy aircraft spiral down out of the haze. The enemy aircraft made a 270-degree turn and headed northeast. Captain Norley opened fire from long range but obtained no strikes. Although Captain Norley was indicating 325mph, the enemy aircraft pulled away and would have escaped, but for some reason the enemy pilot made a diving left turn and the P-51 closed in. Captain Norley fired a short burst and the Me 163 did a 360-degree port turn. While the enemy aircraft rate of turn was surprising, Captain Norley was able to hold deflection and got strikes in the tail of the Me 163. The enemy aircraft slowed up perceptibly and Captain Norley overshot. Pulling around, Captain Norley attacked the enemy aircraft again from astern and obtained more strikes in the tail unit. The enemy aircraft rolled over on its back and went straight in, crashing in a small town.

'The jet encountered by Captain Glover had square wing tips while that in combat with Captain Norley had round wing tips. Both resembled the provisional silhouette in other respects, but seemed larger than expected. All the Me 163s observed were flying singly and their attacks were individual and apparently without co-ordination.'

Some Me 163s had a narrow escape. This sequence of photographs was taken with the gun camera fitted to Captain W H Anderson's P-51 of the 335th FS led by Captain Norley. Although damaged, the Me 163 was not shot down
(*JG 400 Archive*)

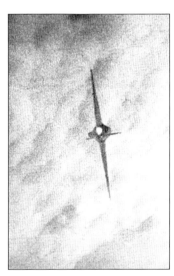

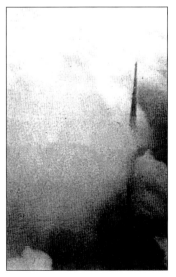

The following observations were made by a bombardier, navigator, and other crew members of the 493rd BG who were in the low squadron of that group during attacks made on it by six Me 163s at 1223 hrs in the vicinity of 5105N-1200E. The attacks were made singly and lasted for about seven minutes. The bombardier and navigator watched four attacks by a single Me 163 and reported;

'An Me 163 was first sighted high, 1,000 feet above the formation whose altitude was 28,000 feet, at 8 o'clock, by the bombardier. The bombardier's attention was caught by the large, cylindrical snowy, fleecy, persistent following vapour trail which did not resemble a bomber or fighter contrail since they are flat and a dull greyish colour. The enemy aircraft was about 1,500 yards off at 8 o'clock, flying parallel to and in the same direction as the formation. It broke into a pursuit curve at this aircraft from 9:30 high, coming in to about 600 yards level, towards the 9 o'clock position, where it pulled into a steep vertical climb, making a wide sweeping turn to the left, completing a circle and pulling into position parallel with the formation which was vulnerable to enemy fire for an estimated seven seconds [*sic*]. The enemy fired one short burst and one sustained burst of about four seconds. Observer thought there were four machine guns, two in each wing. It was thought that machine guns were employed since the muzzle flash was extremely rapid. Bombardier fired about 30 rounds from the nose turret during this attack.

'On the second pass at the formation, the Me 163, flying level about 1,500 yards, came in at 9 o'clock completing a right sharp diving turn, after coming in to within 800 yards of the B-17 formation, going under the squadron about 900 feet and coming out at 5 o'clock, disappearing into cloud cover in this area. Power of the Me 163 was used intermittently but observer estimated a varying speed between 400 to 600mph indicated. This attack lasted about five seconds. It is unknown whether enemy aircraft fired during this attack. Both the tail and ball turret gunners fired at the Me 163 with no apparent damage noted.

'An Me 163, and it was unknown whether it was the original attacker, suddenly appeared out of cloud cover about 1,000 yards out and 1,200 feet below this formation coming in... at 5 o'clock. At about 600 yards, the enemy aircraft turned slightly left from its collision course, but continued the climb, past the formation to an 8 o'clock position about 1,200 yards to the left of the formation, completing a 360 at this point and taking up a position parallel to the squadron. The enemy aircraft came up to the 10 o'clock position where he broke into a diving, turning attack towards 6 o'clock where the aircraft disappeared into cloud cover. Observer reports that C squadron was not flying a particularly tight formation during the encounters. Other aeroplanes in the formation were firing during these and other attacks. Shortly after the fourth attack by the Me 163, a lone Fw 190 made a weak attack at 5 o'clock from 900 yards and then disappeared. All of the attacks described, took place within five minutes.'

Ethell's research revealed that the following USAAF aircraft were attacked during this bombing raid;

B-17 (LL-N, 1st Lt Lorne E Marlott), 91st BG, attacked.
B-17 (LL-O, Lt Bernhard H Allison), 91st BG, attacked.
B-17 (??-???333, 1st Lt William H Trent), 91st BG, attacked.

Leutnant Günter Andreas, 2./JG 400, later recalled the sortie he made that day and the attack on him made by Captain Fred N Glover;

'I have to admit that I was generally lucky while flying the Me 163 because the rocket motor never once failed me on all the occasions I made sharp take-offs (about 20-30). Therefore, I regard my only interesting flight as the one which took place when I was scrambled to intercept the enemy and was shot down!

'This occurred in November 1944 as enemy bombers were heading for Leipzig. All the pilots from the Group, after being briefed for the attack, were immediately taken by lorry to the end of the runway where the Me 163s had been prepared for take-off. Each pilot had his own aircraft. We quickly donned our flying suits and a few minutes later we were sitting in our cockpits ready for take-off. I was in the second aircraft behind my *Staffelkapitän* [Hauptmann Otto Böhner]. We received the signal from the tower to start the turbines but mine refused to start, even though I had pressed the starter button several times. Thirty seconds later, we received the order to take-off but I still couldn't start the turbine.

'In the meantime, it had been discovered that my mechanic had forgotten to connect my aircraft to the power generator cart. The turbine started once the connection had been made and I called the tower to say that I was now ready. I was told to wait to allow the other Me 163s, whose engines had already been running for some time, to pass me before I, almost the last, was finally given permission to start. After take-off, I immediately turned on to the course given by ground control.

'During the climb towards Leipzig I saw contrails and informed ground control that I could proceed on course without further directions. Shortly afterwards, I spotted groups of bombers flying at about 6,000 metres. I climbed above them to about 10,000 metres and throttled the engine back to idle to conserve my fuel in case I needed it

Oberfeldwebel Jakob Bollenrath (right) volunteered to serve for 12 years with the Luftwaffe and began service as a recruit on 1 November 1935. He began training as a pilot on 1 February 1936 with the *Flieger-Ersatzabteilung* 14 in Detmold, continuing his instruction with the *Fliegerschule* in Celle until 1 June 1937. This was followed by training as a flying instructor from June 1937 to May 1944 when he joined EKdo 16. On completion of his training with EKdo 16 he was posted to 2./JG 400 at Venlo. Jakob Bollenrath had two younger brothers: Hubert Bollenrath, who was killed during the advance into Russia on 17 August 1941 and Heinrich, who died from severe injuries while serving with an artillery unit on 20 July 1944. Unbeknown to Jakob, his father repeatedly begged Jakob's commanding officer not to send his son to the Front. His father referred to the Führer's decree, which said that, when two sons from the same family had been killed in the war, the third son should no longer be involved in the fighting. The head of the *Ausbildungskommando der Fluglehrerschule der Luftwaffe*, Hauptmann Buchheim, responded to this plea by saying that Jakob Bollenrath was only serving as an instructor. Jakob persisted with his request to serve on the front line and his wish was rewarded by his transfer to EKdo 16 and later to 2./JG 400. He was shot down and killed on 2 November 1944 by Captain Louis H Norley, 335th FS, 4th FG (far right). Thereby the Bollenrath family lost their third and last son (*JG 400 Archive*)

Oberfeldwebel Herbert Straznicky (right) and Oberfeldwebel Horst Rolly (far right), here both photographed as a Feldwebel, both lost their lives on 2 November. Straznicky was shot down and Rolly's aircraft caught fire soon after take-off. He baled out but his parachute failed to open. Rolly was credited with 36 victories while serving with JG 5 '*Eismeer*' (*JG 400 Archive*)

for an emergency. At this height, I set course for a tail attack on a B-17 that was flying a little to one side of the main formation of bombers. I opened fire when within range and received, almost instantaneously, return fire from the tail gunner, some of his shells hitting the cockpit. My guns fell silent. The canopy was punctured and I noticed that the armoured glass panel in front of me was pock-marked from three of his shells. I was not injured apart from a small cut over my right eye caused by a fragment from the canopy.

'I immediately broke off my attack and attempted to jettison the canopy in case I had to bale out should the aircraft start to burn. At 600km/h the canopy would not budge – it had probably been jammed by the enemy's return fire. I manoeuvred to reduce my speed to about 250km/h and then managed, by using my right arm, to release the canopy. Just as the canopy flew off I came under fire from an enemy fighter and my aircraft, because I had so little speed, nosed over and went into a dive. I attempted to pull out of the dive but realised that the control wires must have been severed in the attack because I could move the control column in all directions without any effect. I decided to bale out but the first three attempts were unsuccessful because the Me 163 had begun to dive more steeply and its drag was too high. I finally baled out at a height of 5,000-6,000 metres after the Me 163 had gained speed and had begun to pull itself out of the dive. I released my parachute and landed in a village close to Wurzen. My aircraft crashed and exploded.'

Oberfeldwebel Bollenrath, 1./JG 400, was shot down by fighters that had followed him back to the airfield. His aircraft exploded close to Zeititz, a village at the eastern end of the runway. The aircraft was claimed by Captain Louis H Norley, 335th FS, 4th FG. Bollenrath was flying Me 163B Wk-Nr. 440003 BQ+UF.

Unteroffizier Rolf Glogner;

'Oberfeldwebel Horst Rolly, 2./JG 400, also suffered an engine flame-out during take-off for a combat sortie. He baled out at a height of 100 metres but the parachute did not open before he hit the ground. He was still alive but did not regain consciousness before he died. He had been wearing one of the new, reefed parachutes that opened gradually and would, therefore, not be torn apart at high speeds.'

Rolly was killed while he was flying Me 163B, Wk-Nr. 440007, BQ+UJ. Rolly was the son of a professor and the last of four brothers.

Schiebeler was flying Me 163B 'White 3' when he engaged three formations of B-17s and two Mustangs over Merseburg. This was his last operational sortie. He took off at 1216 hrs and landed at 1234 hrs.

Oberfeldwebel Herbert Straznicky, 1./JG 400, was reported missing in the Halle-Leipzig area. He was later found dead near Delitzsch, Me 163B WK-Nr. 440186 TP+TN 'White 8' destroyed. Bott recalled, '"Niki" was missed after a combat sortie and a search lasting ten days was made for him within a radius of 40km from the airfield. On the last day he was found 30km away but he could only be identified by his scarf and his EK II medal ribbon. Only small pieces of his aircraft were found. Probably, he was shot down.'

Pictured below, from left to right, Feldwebel Schametz, 2./JG 400, Unteroffizier Anton Steidl and Unteroffizier Kurt Schiebeler who both served with 1./JG 400, and Unteroffizier Ludwig Schweiger who served with I./JG 400 and was reported missing in 1945 after taking off in a Fw 190 from Prague. According to Kurt Schiebeler, Schweiger was not trained to fly the Fw 190 and crashed in a cemetery (*JG 400 Archive*)

Unteroffizier Georg Neher, 2./JG 400, seated in the cockpit of Me 163B Wk-Nr. 191116. This aircraft was allotted the call sign SC+VO, and was tested as a glider by Karl Voy at the Junkers factory at Oranienburg on 20 November 1944. Note that the gun port has been sealed with a fabric patch, indicating that the aircraft was fitted with 30 mm MK 108 cannon (the barrels of the 20 mm MG 151 machine guns projected forward of the wing root fairings) (*JG 400 Archive*)

A memorandum distributed on 12 November ordered the renumbering of JG 400's *Staffeln* and the establishment of new *Staffeln* at the same time. The order took effect immediately. Consequently, 3./JG 400 was renumbered 5./JG 400 and 4./JG 400 became 6./JG 400. The new *Staffeln* were *Stab* II./JG 400, 3./JG 400 and 7./JG 400.

Stab II./JG 400, 5./, 6./ and 7./JG 400 were to be transferred to Stargard. The 'new' third *Staffel* was to be based at Brandis and a 'new' fourth squadron (4./JG 400) was not established. The juggling of the squadron numbers later created much confusion, even among the pilots' Luftwaffe personnel records which relate the 'old' squadron numbers to aircrew who transferred to Stargard.

The commanders of 5./, 6./ and 7./JG 400 were given the acting rank of *Staffelführer*. Their rank, as *Staffelkapitän*, according to Luftwaffe records was not confirmed until February 1945!

On 27 December 1944, Major Wolfgang Späte was appointed *Geschwaderkommodore* of JG 400. Hauptmann Rudolf Opitz took command of II./JG 400 at Stargard at about this time. Hauptmann Wilhelm Fulda was promoted to command I./JG 400 and Hauptmann Albert Falderbaum became *Staffelkapitän* of 1./JG 400.

On 14 February 1945, orders were issued by the *Oberkommando der Luftwaffe* to disband not only *Erprobungskommando* 16 but also *Erprobungskommandos* 26, Ju 388 and Do 335. The order was to be carried out by the KdE.

All flying personnel were placed at the disposal of the generals commanding the different branches of the Luftwaffe and non-flying personnel were either transferred to the *Feldwerft-Ersatzabteilung* at Eschwege, to Luftwaffe regiments or to German Army parachute and infantry regiments. The aircraft were handed over to the Luftwaffe's Quartermaster General for disposal and the tasks which remained to be completed by EKdo 16 were transferred to JG 400.

Albert Falderbaum, flying instructor and German aerobatic champion, joined the Luftwaffe in 1934. After the outbreak of war he continued as a flying instructor with the training school at Brandenburg-Briest. He was promoted to Hauptmann in July 1943. In October-November 1944, he trained to fly the Me 163 with *Ergänzungsstaffel*/JG 400 at Brandis, afterwards joining 1./JG 400 and succeeding Hauptmann Olejnik as *Staffelkapitän* of 1./JG 400 in December, and Hauptmann Fulda as *Gruppenkommandeur* of I./JG 400 in February 1945 (*EN Archive*)

Hauptmann Wilhelm Fulda was awarded the *Ritterkreuz* on 14 June 1941 for his action as commander of a transport glider group during an attack on the Corinthian Isthmus, Greece. From August 1941 to December 1944, he served with: 3./LLG 1; 17./KGzbV 1; 1. *Gotha-Staffel*/KGrzbV 1; as staff officer with 1./LLG 2; *Ergänzungsgruppe* (S) 1; as technical officer, *Stab*/JG 301; as *Staffelkapitän*, 9./JG 301; as *Gruppenkommandeur*, II./JG 301; with the *Sichtungsstelle des Generals der Jagdflieger*; as *Kommodore der Ergänzungsjagdgruppe*; II./JG 4, and as *Gruppenkommandeur*, I./JG 302. Fulda was promoted to *Gruppenkommandeur*, I./JG 400, in January 1945 until the *Gruppe* was disbanded in April. He led the remnants of I./JG 400 who served as infantry in the area between Eger (Cheb) Czechoslovakia and Schirnding from April to May 1945 (*EN Archive*)

Despite the orders for EKdo 16's disbandment, flight tests continued to be made at Brandis and it is on record that Ingenieur Unteroffizier Harald Kuhn flew BV 40 in March and again in April. The last flight he made was with Me 163B V45 on 8 April 1945. All of these flights were made to check the aircraft after they had undergone maintenance and/or had been repaired.

Feldwebel Gerhard Mohr, 1./JG 400, was killed on 10 February 1945 in a crash during an operational sortie; Me 163B-0 Wk-Nr. 440184, DS+VV 'White 2', was destroyed. Mühlstroh recalled;

'Bott was Duty Officer. We [Mühlstroh, Bott and Mohr] were having a mid-day break in the pilots' mess, when we received the order to scramble from JG 400's command post, which was located three kilometres away from the airfield. There were eight aircraft ready for combat. Although my aircraft stood in the third row, I jumped into the first aircraft, which was normally flown by Bott, only to discover that the gunsight was not working. Consequently, Mohr was told to take off first and was last heard giving his altitude as 5,000 metres. I followed and shot out through the cloud cover at 7,000 metres and climbed to 10,000 metres. There were no enemy aircraft in sight.

'We were then told to land immediately. I began a gliding descent at 350km/h but could not see the airfield because of the cloud cover. I was

Throughout January 1945 there was much snow and a few days of good flying weather but there was also a shortage of fuel. Some of the pilots took time to relax, and here, from left to right, are Unteroffizier Georg Neher, Feldwebel Gerhard Mohr, Unteroffizier Kurt Schiebeler, Oberfeldwebel Kristoph Kurz and Oberfeldwebel 'Jupp' Mühlstroh (*JG 400 Archive*)

told to fly a 360-degree course and was then informed that I was over the airfield. I requested clarification of my position but received no answer: the command post's radio had been switched off. In the meantime, I had gained speed and was descending at 800-900km/h and so I pulled up again to reduce my speed back to 350km/h. I then caught a glimpse of the ground and, to port, some He 177s which were parked along the southern perimeter of the airfield. Finally, I saw the

Oberfeldwebel Wilhelm Josef 'Jupp' Mühlstroh, 1./JG 400, being assisted into the cockpit (*JG 400 Archive*)

airfield itself and made a landing, skidding across the runway and finally coming to rest immediately in front of the control tower.'

According to Bott, 'Jupp' Mühlstroh was flying 'White 12' on this occasion. This was Bott's own aircraft and, according to him, it had exceptionally good performance characteristics.

The USAAF 8th Air Force bombed Leipzig on 15 March during which an escort fighter piloted by Captain Ray S Wetmore, 370th FS, 359th FG encountered two Me 163s.

Wetmore's report reads;

'I was leading Red Section escorting bombers southwest of Berlin when I saw two Me 163s circling at about 20,000 feet 20 miles away in the

Me 163B Wk-Nr. 190598 'White 10' was flown twice by Leutnant Hans-Ludwig Löscher during the last week of February 1945. Löscher had by then completed his training with 14./EJG 2 and had been posted to 1./JG 400. 'White 10' was from the first batch of aircraft to be delivered by Junkers (*JG 400 Archive*)

vicinity of Wittenberg. I flew over towards them, and while at 25,000 feet, started after one a little below me. When I got within 3,000 yards, he saw me, turned on his jet, and went up into a 70-degree climb. At about 26,000 feet, his jet quit so he split-essed. I dived with him and levelled off at 2,000 feet on him at six o'clock. During the dive my IAS was between 550 and 600mph. I opened fire at 200 yards. Pieces flew off all over. He made a sharp turn to the right, and I gave him another short burst, and half his left wing flew off, and the aeroplane caught on fire. The pilot baled out, and I saw the enemy aircraft crash into the ground. I claim one (1) Me 163 destroyed in air.'

A photo-reconnaissance sortie was made on 16 March by a Mosquito from No 544 Sqn RAF. The Mosquito XVI NS795, was flown by Flg Off R M Hays and Flt Sgt M Phillips based at RAF Benson. The squadron's operations log book recorded;

'Gotha and Lutzendorf [*sic*, Lützkendorf] targets photographed then attacked by three Me 163s. Aircraft shot up and landed at Lille.'

This brief entry was also recorded in more detail;

'Flg Off R M Hays DFC and Flt Sgt M Phillips had targets at Gotha, Chemnitz and Lutzendorf. Subsequently Lutzendorf and Gotha were claimed. At 1145 hrs, flying at 30,000 feet making a photographic run (with the navigator in the nose of the aircraft) on course 090 degrees over Leipzig, the pilot saw two Me 163s practically at ground level and climbing rapidly. The pilot altered course 90 degrees and opened up fully.

'Within three to five minutes both enemy aircraft were at Mosquito height (30,000 feet) and split up, one to starboard and one to port and slightly above, from which positions they attacked the Mosquito simultaneously on either beam. The pilot did a half-roll and dived vertically, attaining an IAS of 480mph pulling out at 12,000 feet. The pilot then saw that three Me 163's were attacking, one on either beam approximately 500 yards from the Mosquito and the third the same

Informal and formal photographs of Oberfeldwebel Friedrich Ferdinand Helmut Reukauf, who lost his life while flying an Me 163, 15 March 1945. According to official records, the accident was caused by a technical defect. Reukauf was born on 24 January 1912 at Grumbach, near Schmalkalden, Thüringen (*JG 400 Archive*)

distance astern, and all enemy aircraft slightly above. The pilot did not see the enemy aircraft fire but the navigator did. A steep diving turn was made to starboard at deck level where the pilot remained losing sight of the enemy aircraft.

'As the Mosquito levelled off at deck level the pilot saw his starboard engines smoking and without power – presumably as a result of a hit by cannon shells from the Me 163s. This engine was then feathered and the pilot climbed to 2,000 feet and set course for the Allied lines on course 270 degrees. After approximately 30 to 40 minutes flying the navigator saw a single Me 109 approaching from 1,000 yards astern and at approximately 2,400 feet. The Mosquito then dived to deck level again and then flew up and down valleys pinpointed as being approximately 30 miles west of Kassel. During this evasive action the Me 109 was lost to sight and made no further contact.

'Approximately 45 minutes later while still at deck level, the Mosquito crossed a small unidentified town and experienced intense flak – the Mosquito sustained hits and the navigator was injured in the foot. Shortly afterwards the pilot again climbed to 2,000 feet to clear high ground and to take advantage of three-tenths/five-tenths pre-frontal cloud (Cu). After flying for about 30 minutes American C-47s and gliders were seen on the ground through a break in the cloud (these aircraft were not on an airfield) and the pilot decided to carry on.

'At this stage the course was altered to 300 degrees encountering ten-tenths frontal conditions with rain. The VHF set was turned on and Mayday calls made on all the channels without result. The pilot flew in these conditions for about one hour estimating that by this time he had cleared all high ground and then descending broke cloud at 800 feet and later pinpointed Lille. A normal single-engined approach was made to Lille/Vendeville airfield.

'The pilot was unaware that the starboard tyre was punctured by cannon shells and as soon as he touched down the aircraft swung violently to starboard, both port and starboard undercarriage legs collapsed, and the Mosquito was severely damaged. Inspection of the aircraft revealed damage by cannon shells – presumably from the Me 163s. One shell passed through the starboard engine nacelle, another through the starboard engine near the boss, damaging and fracturing the glycol tank. A flak shell also hit the blade of the starboard propeller, spraying the fuselage and starboard engine with fragments. For this excellent display of courage and determination the pilot, Flg Off R M Hays had an immediate award of the Distinguished Flying Cross. The navigator was taken to hospital at Lille.'

Unteroffizier Rolf Glogner;

'I shot down a Mosquito on 16 March 1945. In this case, Göring should have awarded me a medal and given me promotion and special leave. Instead, I received confirmation of my victories in Russia. Because, up to that time, I had only received the gold *Frontflug-Spange für Jäger*, I was retrospectively awarded an EK II. Shortly afterwards I was promoted to Feldwebel.

'After I./JG 400 was disbanded in Brandis, I was transferred to JG 7 at Prague-Ruzyne. It was there that I learnt from Fritz Kelb that I had been awarded the EK I.'

At the beginning of April, Major Späte was ordered to join III./JG 7 at Alt-Lönnewitz. Späte took over command as *Gruppenkommandeur* from Rudi Sinner who was injured in combat on 4 April, 1945.

Bott recalled the then-prevailing situation and his service with *Kommando Elbe* between 6 and 8 April;

'In the autumn of 1944, the RLM had forbidden Me 163 sorties, as each one had resulted in a loss of 30% of its pilots. Attacks on bombers were forbidden but those on reconnaissance aircraft were allowed. Consequently, the 90 [*sic*] or so aircraft on the site were dispersed and hidden in the woods and fields surrounding the airfield. Afterwards, the pilots became lethargic, no longer volunteering enthusiastically to conduct test flights but rather trying to get out of doing so.

'The situation changed with a call for volunteers from Brandis to fly combat missions against the bombers. Hauptmann Fulda and nine other pilots, including Löscher and I, responded to the call. Five were selected from Brandis and sent to Stendal, where they were joined by pilots from other squadrons. Altogether 250 men volunteered for duty under the command of Oberst Hajo Herrmann. We were assembled on the parade ground and told that we would use our aircraft to ram enemy bomber formations. We were to fly stripped-down Me 109s in flights of four aircraft at a height of 11,000 metres and there await the arrival of the bombers. It was hoped that the suddenness of our attacks would lead to success and would have a positive effect on negotiations between Germany and the Allies at the end of the war, which then seemed to be inevitable. We were given instruction by "specialists" in ramming techniques. Not very convincing.

'Sixty pilots were sent from Stendal to each of three airfields. I was sent to Gardelegen with three other pilots from Brandis. Fifteen *Schwärme* [Flights] were formed and I was given command of

Unteroffizier Rolf 'Bubi' Glogner served with 2./JG 400 and was the youngest Me 163 pilot, earning him the nickname 'Bubi'. He was promoted to Feldwebel in March 1945. On 16 March 1945, he and Feldwebel Ernst Schelper from the same squadron took off to intercept the Mosquito flown by Flg Off Hays and Flt Sgt Phillips but Feldwebel Schelper was forced to turn back because he could not jettison the undercarriage dolly. The Mosquito jettisoned its drop tanks and these flew past Unteroffizier Glogner as he pressed home his attack. After he had fired a few rounds, his MK 108 cannon jammed but the shells he did fire hit the Mosquito's starboard engine. According to Hays and Phillips' combat report, other Me 163s were involved in the attack but the names of their pilots have not been discovered, although it has been reported that Flieger Walter Dittmar flying an Me 163 equipped for ramming operations took part in this action. Unteroffizier Glogner served with SG 101 and JG 52 in Russia before he was transferred to EKdo 16 and JG 400. He was awarded the *Frontflug-Spange* in Gold and the *Eisernes Kreuz* 2nd and 1st Class. Glogner scored three victories. During April 1945 he joined Major Späte at JG 7, based at Prague-Ruzyne, but never flew the Me 262 (*JG 400 Archive*)

Schwarm 11. With little warning, we were ordered to scramble on 7 April 1945. Only 40 Me 109s were available. My brand new Me 109G-14 was delivered half an hour after we had been ordered into combat but I was not allowed to make another flight with it so soon after it had landed. In the afternoon, I flew the aircraft to Stendal and reported to Oberst Herrmann. He told me that similar operations were being planned against bombers flying over Bavaria and that I should fly the Me 109 there. I prepared to take off but in the end was not allowed to do so, as the aircraft was to remain in Stendal and be blown up.

'I then asked Oberst Herrmann for permission for the four of us to return to Brandis, where we had some Me 163s in storage, so that we could attempt to obtain permission from the *Jagddivision* to fly a combat sortie. We were given the necessary permission, and aircraft for seven of us were prepared for combat at Brandis. On the day before we would have completed our preparations, however, we received an order to disband JG 400 and join the German Army. Brandis also received the order to blow up its aircraft.'

The last combat sortie of I./JG 400 before the end of the war was made on 10 April against a force of 230 RCAF Halifaxes and Lancasters which attacked Mockau and Engelsdorf. The post-mission operational narrative reported;

'Target Mockau. No cloud. Visibility was excellent. Crews were able to visually identify the target by the railway and the wooded area. Bombing was carried out either visually or on yellow T/Is [target indicators] as instructed by the M/B [master bomber], who was clearly heard. Results appeared accurate and concentrated. Dust and smoke rising to 5,000 feet were observed. The M/B instructed early crews to overshoot the markers.

'Slight H/F [heavy Flak] was seen, mostly accurately predicted, bursting at 16/18,000 feet. Approximately eight aircraft were damaged by flak. Several Me 163s were sighted in the target area. There were at least two combats reported, with one Me 163 claimed as damaged.

'Target Engelsdorf. Weather was clear with excellent visibility. Crews were able to map read to the target and to visually identify the aiming point. Bombing was carried out visually or on red T/Is from 15/18,000 feet. The M/B was clearly heard. He instructed early crews to overshoot the markers by one second and later by three seconds. A good concentration of bombing was built up around the aiming point. Smoke and dust were seen rising up to 10,000 feet. Two large explosions were noted, one of these emitting black oily smoke. Many fires were seen through the smoke. Railway sheds south of the A/P [approach path] received direct hits. Crews considered the attack produced excellent results.

'Slight H/F, most accurately predicted, was seen bursting at 16/18,000 feet. Several aircraft were damaged by flak. Some were seen shot down in the target area including one Mustang and one jet propelled aircraft. Several Me 262s and at least one Me 163 were sighted in the target area but no combats were reported. All aircraft attempted photos and those so far developed show good detail.'

The day's events are described in *The RCAF Overseas. The Sixth Year*;

'The Halifaxes began their seven-minute blitz on Mockau, marred only by the error of one group of kites which bombed the Lancaster target. Otherwise the attack paralleled the first. Here too most of the through lines and siding tracks were out; much rolling stock was knocked about, and round-houses, repair shops and sheds, as well as factory buildings in the vicinity, were destroyed or severely damaged. Heavy flak was slight over both targets. A few enemy fighters were seen, but only one combat was reported. One bomber was missing from each force.

'The Lancaster contingent lost a freshman crew from the *Porcupines* (No 433 Sn) – Plt Off R J Grisdale, Flg Offs I Zierler and H G McLeod, Flt Sgts J M Hirak, F G Seeley and D W Roberts and Sgt W A Thurston (RAF). A veteran Halifax crew of the *Swordfish* squadron (No 415 Sqn) was composed of Flg Offs R S Evans, L M Spry, L E Veitch, Flt Sgts M J Burns, D L Lorens and R D Teevin and Sgt J M Andrews (RAF).

'The sole encounter with enemy fighters brought a Distinguished Service Order (DSO) to Sqn Ldr C H Mussels, DFC of the *Vancouvers* (No 405 Sqn). He had just completed his first run over the target when an Me 163 attacked and with one burst shot away the rear turret and starboard rudder. The port rudder was smashed and both elevators were badly damaged. The rear gunner, Flt Lt M L Mellstrom, is believed to have been killed by the fighter's first deadly burst. The Lancaster began to dive out of control and, as the trimming controls were useless, Mussels had a desperate struggle before he was able to level out. To keep the nose up it was necessary to lash the control column back.

'Escorted by Mustangs, which had provided fighter cover for both operations, Mussels flew his crippled bomber back to Britain. After crossing the coast he ordered his crew to bale out of the aircraft. Four did so, but the mid-upper gunner, Plt Off R T Dale, had been seriously wounded and was unable to leave. Mussels remained with his comrade, flew to the nearest airfield and then, although his flaps were useless and the control column was still lashed back, he made a superbly skilful landing.'

The bombers were accompanied by a fighter escort drawn from No 309 (Polish) Sqn.

Feldwebel Hans Hoever;

'I watched Kelb attack a formation of about 150 Lancasters that were bombing Leipzig and the city's outskirts on 10 April. I had just finished my shift and was standing on the observation tower of the fighter control command post next to the *Würzburg* radar when I heard over the loudspeaker that Leutnant Kelb was about to take off with his special aircraft. I heard the rocket motor and saw Kelb climb above the trees at the end of the runway south of where I was standing. I followed him with the aid of the long-range Flak telescope and saw him head towards the lead aircraft of the bomber formation which was flying at a height of about 8,000 metres. I thought he wanted to ram it but just at the moment as he passed about 100 metres below the aircraft, the bomber exploded in a cloud of smoke and flames. I had never before seen a bomber so easily destroyed as that attacked by Leutnant Kelb.

'Just after the bomber exploded I noticed that the escort fighters had spotted Kelb. My first thought was that he had enough fuel left, at least enough for 15 seconds, to re-ignite his engine. I was pleased to see the motor spring to life just as the fighters swarmed down to attack him and Kelb shoot through them to a height 2,000 metres above them. My telescope allowed me to follow the ensuing fight. With his fuel spent, Kelb turned and dived past a fighter that was close to him with such a speed that the fighter was not aware of what had happened. About two hours later, I listened to the debriefing given by the *Kommandeur*, Hauptmann Fulda, to the squadron's officers standing around him.'

From a summary of the work carried out at *Fliegerhorst* Brandis in the final weeks of the war up to and including 12 April, 1945;

'The first (and also the last) operational trial of *Jägerfaust* [a recoilless weapon which fired shells vertically upwards from a rifled barrel] was made over Leipzig on 10 April 1945. At about 1800 hrs a strong formation of enemy bombers appeared over the city. A Me 163B with "vertical armament" went into action. The aircraft came unheeded below the enemy machines. The armament was immediately discharged. A Boeing B-17 [*sic*, Lancaster] at once fell out of the sky like a burning torch, none of the crew being able to make their escape. Two other aircraft were so badly damaged that they also crashed after flying over our airfield. Our aircraft was able to draw away still unobserved by the enemy, and was only located and attacked by Mustang and Thunderbolt fighters when it had arrived back over our airfield. The anti-aircraft defences were able to keep the enemy aircraft at a distance, while a smooth landing was made with no damage to our aircraft. These were the last successes obtained with the Me 163B.'

The irony of the attack was that the bombers destroyed the factory where the *Jägerfaust* was being made.

Leutnant Friedrich 'Fritz' Kelb, who served with 2./JG 400, is seen here climbing into Junkers-built Me 163B Wk-Nr. 190579. On 10 April 1945, he made the first and also the last operational attack with an Me 163 fitted with the *Jägerfaust*. He destroyed an RCAF Lancaster which was attacking Engelsdorf on the outskirts of Leipzig. The HASAG factory which produced the *Jägerfaust* was destroyed in the bombing. According to the RCAF combat report, three Me 163s were seen climbing from Brandis. The identity of the aircraft which Leutnant Kelb flew on this occasion is not known. At least three Me 163Bs were fitted with the *Jägerfaust* (*JG 400 Archive*)

The wreckage of Me 163B V45
Wk-Nr. 16310054 C1+05 ex-PK+QP at
Brandis. The aircraft is believed
to have made its last flight on 8 April
1945, piloted by Flieger-Ingenieur
Harald Kuhn. The aircraft was one
of at least three equipped with the
Jägerfaust, trials of which were
conducted with BV45 on Christmas
Eve 1944. On that occasion the
aircraft was badly damaged. The
remains of a Henschel Hs 130A,
with which Junkers conducted
engine trials at Brandis, can be
seen behind the wreckage of BV45
(*Maj Gen George Ruhlen*)

On 12 April, Späte arrived at Brandis requesting six pilots to fly the Me 262 at Prague. Early the following morning, Kelb, Glogner and Oberfeldwebel August 'Gustl' Müller, with Leutnant Bott in an Bf 110, took off. Georg Neher flew with Oberfeldwebel Kurz in an Arado Ar 234 to Prague-Ruzyne. They had not been given any instructions on how to fly the aircraft. At Prague they were told that they were not wanted. They then flew a Bf 108 to Plattling. Neher was taken prisoner near Mühldorf. Another pilot, who was not chosen to fly the Me 262, took *Nachrichtenhelferinnen* in a Ju 52. Wiedemann, Schiebeler's wingman, did not arrive; he was shot down soon after take-off. Schiebeler returned to Brandis and took off again a little later the same day. Kelb stayed in Prague. The others received orders to transfer to Fürstenfeldbruck. Everyone made his own way there.

The aircraft remaining at Brandis were destroyed by airfield personnel on 14 April. Hauptmann Fulda and the remnants of I./JG 400 (pilots and ground personnel) were ordered to join forces with the German Army. The Group reached an area near Eger (Cheb) and took up defensive positions in the Bohemian Forest on the German-Czechoslovakian border. Most of the Group were taken prisoner on 26 April.

Hans Hoever;

'The Americans were approaching from the west and the Russians from the east. We were ordered to join the German Army and reached Schirnding on the German-Czechoslovakian border, where we fought relentlessly until we had exhausted our ammunition. We suffered heavy losses. When we withdrew there were only a small number of us left, perhaps about 30-40 men, the majority had been killed in the hills around Schirnding.

'The war ended for the remnants of JG 400 at 1600 hrs on 8 May 1945 at Duppau, about 25km to the east of Karlsbad. We received our discharge papers and the remaining vehicles were divided among us so we could make our own way through Germany. We destroyed our weapons and within the hour small groups of us had set off in the same direction. On the following day, I managed to escape to Stollberg near Chemnitz via Joachimsthal by hitching a ride on a German army lorry. My family had been evacuated to Stollberg. Six weeks later my family and I reached Cologne.'

On 16 April, Brandis airfield was captured by Task Force Collins (Lt Col Kenneth W Collins, CO, 60th Armoured Infantry Battalion), Combat Command A (CCA), 9th Armoured Division, US Army. According to US Army After Action Reports, CCA found two intact aircraft and the wreckage of 300(!) aircraft including about 40 Me 163s. The intact aircraft might be Me 163B V13 (Wk-Nr. 16310022 VD+EV) and the Horten IX V1 (Ho 229), both of which were found disassembled in hangars. BV13 was in the process of being modified to Me 163D standard. The Horten IX V1 had been sent to Brandis in March 1945.

The remains of Me 163s were used as backdrops for a number of American soldiers during their occupation of the airfield at Brandis, including Pfc Marvin L Freeman, Anti-Tank Platoon, Headquarters Company, 3rd Battalion, 273rd Infantry Regiment (*Marvin L Freeman*)

II. *GRUPPE/ JAGDGESCHWADER* 400

The *Staffeln* of II./JG 400 were first established in Brandis at the end of September 1944, their transfer to Stargard following at the beginning of October. Leutnant Peter Gerth was ordered to take command of and build up the first *Staffel*, then still designated 3./JG 400. His technical personnel were unfamiliar with the Me 163 and had to receive special training but engine specialists from Walter were made available. Leutnant Reinhard Opitz joined him on 7 October, and Oberleutnant Franz Woidich was appointed *Staffelführer*, 4./JG 400, in September. The following month, the *Staffelführer* of 3./ and 4./JG 400 were changed and Woidich took over 3./JG 400, replacing Gerth, who took over 4./JG 400.

On 12 November an order was issued to renumber these squadrons and with it the establishment of new *Staffeln*. Consequently, 3./JG 400 and 4./JG 400 were numbered 5./JG 400 and 6./JG 400 respectively. To these was added a third *Staffel*, 7./JG 400, which was formed at Stettin-Altdamm. Their commanders were given the acting rank of *Staffelführer*.

Stargard had a broad concrete runway which had been built in a field close to a large country estate to the southwest of this town in Pomerania. The runway was aligned approximately 340 degrees towards Pölitz, where a large synthetic oil plant had been built. Sharp take-offs were to be followed by landings at the airfield at Stargard, from where a road had been built to tow the Me 163 back to the runway.

Leutnant Peter Gerth. From March to October 1944 he trained with EKdo 16 and *Ergänzungsstaffel/ JG 400*, afterwards commanding 6./JG 400, which was transferred from Brandis to Stargard in November 1944. He served with that unit as *Staffelführer/Staffelkapitän* until May 1945 (*JG 400 Archive*)

Left
Leutnant Reinhard Opitz joined the Luftwaffe in 1941 as an officer cadet. In 1942, he trained as a pilot at the *Luftkriegsschule* II, Berlin-Gatow and, in 1943, underwent fighter pilot training at the *Zerstörerschule* II, Neubiberg. He was promoted to Leutnant in June 1943. Opitz served with ZG 101 until August 1944 as an operational pilot and fighter pilot instructor, claiming two aircraft destroyed; Opitz was himself shot down in February 1944. He transferred to *Ergänzungsstaffel/ JG 400* at Brandis in August 1944, and with II./JG 400 to Stargard, becoming *Staffelführer* 7./JG 400 at Stettin-Altdamm in November 1944, and *Staffelkapitän* 7./JG 400 in February 1945. Leutnant Opitz transferred with his squadron to Husum via Salzwedel and Nordholz in February 1945. He helped to dismantle the Me 163s at Husum at the end of war and was held as a prisoner of war from June 1945 until his release in 1946 (*Reinhard Opitz*)

Right
Oberleutnant Franz Woidich joined 5./JG 27 in July 1941 as Oberfähnrich, serving in North Africa (credited with two victories). In April 1942 he transferred to 3./JG 52 on the Eastern Front where, in June 1943, Woidich was promoted to *Staffelkapitän*. He was awarded the *Deutsches Kreuz* on 6 December 1943 and at the end of 1943 he was credited with 56 victories. Woidich became *Staffelkapitän*, 5.(*Sturm*)/ JG 4, in May 1944 and was awarded the *Ritterkreuz* on 9 June 1944 (80 victories). Woidich started training on the Me 163 with *Ergänzungsstaffel/*JG 400 on 11 August 1944 and afterwards joined 4./JG 400 (renumbered 6./JG 400) at Brandis in September. He was transferred to 5./JG 400 in October and served the squadron as *Staffelführer/Staffelkapitän* until April 1945. Woidich ended the war credited with 110 victories (107 claimed on Eastern Front) (*JG 400 Archive*)

The squadron's equipment and accommodation were new. Materiel arrived from every quarter and also specialists, among whom were *Luftnachrichtenoffiziere* [signals officers] who were to guide the aircraft to their targets. This materiel included a completely equipped mobile workshop, a number of 3½-ton Opel Blitz tankers with special attachments for *T-Stoff* and *C-Stoff*, all of the necessary radio-navigation equipment and, finally, the aircraft, which had been carefully packed for transport by rail. The Group's quarters were not ready and what was available was very primitive. At that time the *Fliegerhorst* Stargard was not occupied by the military personnel: it had been used for some time for the production and storage of torpedoes. The hangars had been converted for this purpose and could not be used for maintenance or as shelters for the Me 163.

By the end of October the *Staffeln* were ready to make the first towed take-offs and to conduct ground tests of the engines which had been installed in the aircraft. At the end of the month Leutnant Reinhard Opitz received a telex from the office of the *General der Jagdflieger* informing him that he was to take over 7./JG 400 and build up the *Staffel* at Stettin-Altdamm. The airfield there was small and, because it was close to the River Oder and the Haff was frozen over, he did consider making sharp take-offs from the ice. This idea could not be carried out, however, simply because the propellant which the *Staffel* had been promised was not available, even for ground testing the engines. However, towed flights were made over Stettin with the Bf 110.

The Me 163 was flown many times at Stargard but only scrambled for combat on three occasions. One of these combat sorties was flown in November 1944 when Leutnant Gerth intercepted a Mosquito, whose contrail had revealed its presence. He attacked the Mosquito from the rear and one of its crew baled out and was taken prisoner. A second Mosquito was seen but it escaped. Gerth believed the Mosquitos had been ordered to fly a reconnaissance sortie over the synthetic oil factory at Pölitz.

According to Gerth, Pölitz was bombed the following day (or the day after that). He and an unteroffizier were scrambled to intercept the bombers, which were flying at 4,000 metres. They climbed to 10,000 metres and from this altitude dived to make two attacks. According to the evidence from Gerth's gun camera, his cannon shells struck a wing of one of the bombers and pieces of the wing flew off. The Flak, however, claimed all four aircraft that had been shot down that day. At the time he made his attack he saw no escort fighters although these had been seen over Stargard before and after the air raid.

Although both Opitz and Gerth generally agree that Pölitz was attacked in November, Opitz implied that the Me 163 was not ready for combat operations by the end of October, and there is no record of the USAAF mounting an attack on Pölitz in November 1944. The RAF mounted night raids on 21/22 December 1944 and on 13/14 January 1945, and the RCAF bombed Pölitz on 8 February 1945. Curiously, the Eighth Air Force lost four B-17G bombers to anti-aircraft fire during the attack it made on Pölitz on 7 October 1944! The 457th BG lost 42-97638 'Z' of the 749th BS, while the 748th lost 42-102905 and 44-6469 'U' and the 750th lost 44-8046 'N'. A fifth B-17G, 43-38529, ditched in the English Channel after the attack.

In February 1945, the Group was informed that it was to abandon Stargard and destroy everything that it had to leave behind. Hauptmann Rudolf Opitz, *Gruppenkommandeur* II./JG 400, flew out in a Bf 110 but it caught fire and he had to make an emergency landing in Stettin. On 1 March, the *Gruppe* was officially ordered to transfer from Stargard to airfields in northwest Germany (Bad Zwischenahn, Wittmundhafen or Nordholz) and from there to operate against four-engined bombers. Aircrew from I./JG 400 were to be used to reinforce the second Group, although the task of I./JG 400 was still to protect the refineries in the vicinity of Brandis as well as train new pilots.

This order seems to be one where the bureaucracy caught up with events, as the *Staffeln* had already evacuated Stargard and Stettin-Altdamm one month earlier. However, it might have applied only to the *Stab* of II./JG 400 as Hauptmann Rudolf Opitz evacuated Stargard airfield at the beginning of March. On 20 February, the Russian front was about 10km to the south of Stargard and the Soviet Army reached the River Oder on 31 March 1945.

Gerth recalled that his *Staffel*, 6./JG 400, moved to Bad Zwischenahn via Stendal at the end of January. 5./JG 400 must have been transferred to Wittmundhafen via Salzwedel at about the same time, as Reinhard Opitz does not recall seeing the *Staffel* on his arrival at Salzwedel.

Leutnant Reinhard Opitz and his *Staffel*, 7./JG 400, left Stettin during the first few days of February 1945 in bitterly cold weather. They had loaded all their equipment and aircraft on the last of the goods trains to be put together under 'normal' conditions. Russian tanks had already reached Schneidemühl, a town 110km away on the southeastern border of Pomerania. A few days later they arrived in

The slowest moving form of transport towing the then-fastest aircraft in the world. The photograph might have been taken at Salzwedel but such a scene was a common sight at other airfields where the Me 163 was based (*JG 400 Archive*)

Salzwedel, where they had been ordered to unload the *Staffel's* aircraft and equipment.

After a brief inspection of the airfield at Salzwedel, Leutnant Opitz realised that this site was also unsuitable for operations with the Me 163. It was too short and there was no concrete runway. Various fighter squadrons came and went during the next few weeks and the *Staffel* could hardly make a move during the day because of the ever-present American fighters. Its aircraft were housed in barns by local farmers.

In the meantime, the *Staffel* had learned how to tow the Me 163 without its wings along the ground by attaching it to a truck with the aid of a short towing-bar: the transport of the Me 163 from the hangar to its point of take-off could not be done under the aircraft's own power. As was to be expected the scarcity of food and war materials at that time naturally meant that petrol also had to be spared. The *Fliegerhorst* at Brandis, like all other German airfields, had a farmer who was responsible for ensuring that the grass was cut short and the airfield kept tidy. Cows were also allowed to graze there for this purpose. This gave the *Horstkommandant* at Salzwedel the idea of ordering the Me 163 to be towed to its starting position by an ox! The ox was provided by an old man who had served in the *Landsturm* (Home Guard) and who kept the airfield in order.

Regular flying in Salzwedel proved to be out of the question: the days were continually interrupted by air-raid warnings and the aircraft and their equipment were so widely dispersed that many kilometres had to be covered daily just to check their status. The arrival of an order to transfer 7./JG 400 to Bad Zwischenahn during the first few days of March allowed the unit to breathe a sigh of relief and gave hope that it would see some action. As part of its preparations for the move, Leutnant Reinhard Opitz flew with Hauptmann Frömert, who was attached to the *Stab* of II./JG 400, to Bad Zwischenahn. There, it was difficult to find a large enough area to land, even with the Fieseler Storch. The American and British bombers had left the airfield in such a mess during an earlier attack that Bad Zwischenahn had to be ruled out for operations by 7./JG 400. Consequently, the

Assistance is given to a pilot prior to take-off at Nordholz (*Reinhard Opitz*)

Sharp take-off, probably at Nordholz. Camouflage markings indicate that the Me 163 was built by Klemm (*JG 400 Archive*)

Junkers-built Me 163B at Nordholz: Wk-Nr. 191329 'Yellow 7' (*JG 400 Archive*)

Staffel received orders to transfer to Nordholz, the old airfield close to Cuxhaven which had been used by Zeppelins during World War 1. The airfield offered all the conditions required to be able to fly operational sorties.

The aircraft were unloaded from the railway wagons immediately after their arrival. As fuel was available 7./JG 400 was able to conduct engine ground tests a few days later. The aircraft were checked out by making towed flights before making sharp take-offs. The preparations for combat, however, were again interrupted by low-flying American and British fighters but the *Staffel* was so busy concentrating on technical and organisational matters that it hardly registered their presence. On top of this the *Staffel* was faced with having to cope with ever-growing numbers of pilots and other Luftwaffe personnel reporting for duty who had been driven out of their bases by the Allied advance northwards.

The Allied advance again made the *Staffel's* position untenable and it was ordered to move to Husum. The transfer from Nordholz to Husum took place between 10 and 15 April. Reinhard Opitz remembered

Junkers-built Me 163B at Nordholz, Wk-Nr. 191454 'Yellow 11' (*JG 400 Archive*)

This aircraft was flown by Leutnant Reinhard Opitz at Nordholz on 10 April. Two days later he flew it to Husum. The stencilled *Werknummer* on the fin, 10061, corresponds to Me 163B V52 Wk-Nr. 16310061. The photograph shows the aircraft marked with the squadron number 'Yellow 1'. This Me 163 was brought to the UK and handed over to the French *Armée de l'Air* in March 1946 (*Reinhard Opitz*)

the move particularly well because it took place without him being given any precise orders as to how it should be made. He had, in the meantime, been able to establish a good relationship with the personnel at the German Navy's stores at Cuxhaven, from where the *Staffel* drew its rations, and used this to good effect by requesting a ship to transport the unit to Husum. Once the formal hurdles had been cleared, the *Staffel* was provided with a coastal freighter which was loaded during the night. The Me 163s with their wings attached were towed behind the *Staffel's* lorries from Nordholz to the harbour at Cuxhaven. The eight or ten aircraft that had previously been made ready for flight were towed by Bf 110s to Husum, as flights proved especially difficult because of the ever-present British and American fighters.

Reinhard Opitz later recalled;

'I kept my Me 163 ready for take-off at the end of the concrete runway at Nordholz until the aircraft had all been loaded onto the ship. Our squadron's mechanic urged me to empty its tanks but I could not decide whether to do this or fly the aircraft to Husum after making a sharp take-off.

'On 12 April, the evening sky appearing empty of British fighters, I took-off in my Me 163 with the squadron marking, "Yellow 1", and climbed to an altitude of almost 13,000 metres where I circled over the mouth of the River Elbe. The distance from there to Husum was about 95 to 100km, and it was clear to me that I could glide to Husum at high speed from that altitude. I navigated using as landmarks the characteristic bays along the North Sea coast and, in particular, just off Husum, the Isle of Nordstrand, which was connected to the mainland by a causeway. I still remember the deep-blue, evening sky and this flight as one of the highlights of my days as a pilot.

'I spotted the airfield at Husum from a height of 3,000 metres and surprised the *Fliegerhorst* by making a high speed flight over the runway at a height of only a few metres. They had become used to Me 163s landing and had been expecting the Bf 110 that usually towed them. I believe this was one of the very few cross-country flights ever made with a Me 163. My log book records that I took-off in Nordholz at 1820 hrs and landed in Husum at 1829 hrs.

'Without doubt our transfer to Husum must be regarded as miraculous, accomplished as it was during the final days of the war punctually and without any real difficulty. Everyone realised that the war would soon end but nobody knew when. We, therefore, re-assembled our aircraft, conducted engine tests and made a series of sharp take-offs.

'One event which we regarded as particularly tragic at the time took place on 14 April. A Feldwebel, who had evaded capture when the Allied Army took the airfield at Rheine and who had managed to make his way to us at Nordholz, was killed soon after taking-off in a Bf 110. He was towing a Me 163 and was shot down by a low-flying British Spitfire, which had managed to approach the airfield unnoticed. The Me 163 crash-landed in a clearing in a pine forest.'

Oberfeldwebel Werner Nelte, the pilot of the Me 163 and who had previously served with I./JG 400 at Brandis, was killed. He was shot down by Sqn Ldr John B Shepherd, DFC and bar, the commanding officer of No 41 Sqn, No 125 Wing, RAF.

II./JG 400 was officially disbanded on 20 April 1945. The order was to be put into effect immediately and required confirmation by 1 May that it had been carried out.

At the beginning of 1945, radar coverage over northern Germany had been well-organised but, because of various problems, it was in disarray by April. The unit received reports of enemy aircraft approaching from dawn till dusk and, because of the lack of radar directional control, the *Staffel* was forced to take matters into its own hands.

Reinhard Opitz;

'A few days before the end of the war, at about the end of April, we spotted, through a gap in the cloud cover, a contrail from an

Me 163Bs 'Yellow 2' and 'Yellow 13' on the apron at Husum (*EN Archive*)

aircraft flying westwards. Because the contrail could only be from a high-flying British reconnaissance aircraft, two Me 163s were ordered to intercept it. One of the aircraft was flown by Leutnant Gerth (who had transferred back to Husum before his unit surrendered at Bad Zwischenahn). Both aircraft took off and climbed normally, and we could see from their contrails that they were rapidly approaching their target. We also saw muzzle flashes from the cannon faintly way out over the sea but then the aircraft were lost to view and we had to wait for their return to hear what happened.

'The report from Gerth, one of the most experienced of the Me 163 pilots and a fighter pilot who had been accredited with a number of aircraft shot down while flying an Me 109, was typical regarding the technical status of the Me 163. He reported that he had approached the fast-flying Mosquito to within 200 metres below the tail of the aircraft before opening fire. The Me 163's MK 108 cannon each fired one shot before they jammed. The pilot of the Mosquito proved particularly adroit. He knew that if he flew low over the sea both Me 163s would be forced to give up their attack since they would not have enough height to regain their base. Next day we took Gerth's Me 163 to the firing range to check the cannon. These functioned perfectly, and once again seemed to confirm that the forces exerted during manoeuvres immediately led to the ammunition belts jamming in their chutes.'

This attack was made on Mosquito XVI RG131, flown by Flt Lt J M Daniels and WO J Amos of No 544 Sqn RAF based at Benson, Oxfordshire. The crew subsequently recorded their experience;

'We were airborne at base at 0855 hrs on 25 April 1945, and set course for Hannover, having been briefed to photograph targets around Stettiner Bay and at Copenhagen. We climbed on track to [con]trail heights which was 30,000 feet, and descended 1,000 feet so as to fly just below. The sky was clear of cloud but the trail heights kept lowering, until at Hannover we were down to 25,000 feet.

'We reached our first target, Pasewalk aerodrome, at 1050 hrs, and, although four-tenths cumulus had formed, one run was sufficient and we were equally fortunate on our next two targets, Anklam and Tutow aerodromes.

'We then set course for the Kaiser-Fahrt Canal where we were to search for the pocket battleship *Lützow*. Innumerable columns of smoke were rising from the Russian front to a height of 5,000 feet.

'We located our target, noting that the *Lützow* was still in the same position as last reported. Only one run was required and we then set course for Copenhagen.

'As soon as we crossed the coast we passed over a ten-tenths layer of strato cumulus that stretched as far as we could see. This persisted until we reached our ETA Copenhagen, and as there was not a gap to be seen, we set course 259 degrees magnetic for base.

'The cloud began to break up at the Danish western coast and the sea was totally clear. Heligoland appeared on our port quarter. So, deciding to do a run over it, we took one last look around and altered course 20 degrees port. [The crew were then about 30 miles offshore from the Danish coast on a heading of 245 degrees magnetic at 25,000 feet.]

'At that instant I [Daniels] saw two bursts of cannon fire appear low and ahead of the starboard wing tip. Shouting a warning to my navigator I went into a steep turn to port, at the same time opening up to 2,850 revs and full boost. My navigator warned me that an enemy aircraft, apparently an Fw 190, was 500 yards behind and turning in for another attack. I altered my steep turn to starboard. It was then observed that the enemy aircraft was an Me 163. I then began a series of steep turns 180 degrees in arc turning through 270 degrees so as to lead the enemy aircraft further out to sea. This action lasted for approximately seven minutes, during which time the enemy aircraft got in two more bursts of fire, both to starboard. We observed that the enemy aircraft made very little use of its rocket.

'The enemy aircraft then changed its tactics and, diving down, pulled up to attack underneath. My navigator informed me just before the Me 163 attacked and I put the aircraft into a sudden dive. The enemy followed and opened up a continuous burst of fire, which passed overhead, bursting 100 yards in front. I continued to push the stick forward until, at 13,000 feet, the enemy broke away and turned north. Indicated speed was 480mph and the aircraft was shuddering violently. There was a continuous trail coming from the trailing edges of both wings and extending from the root to the wing tip. I brought the aircraft back to straight and level solely by the trimmer and, as the enemy aircraft was not in sight, continued to fly at 2,850 revs plus 12 boost for five minutes. Engine instruments were normal, the only apparent results of the dive being the port boost capsule giving way.

'The balance of the trip was flown at 10,000 feet and proved to be uneventful. We landed at base at 1425 hrs with ten minutes endurance remaining.'

Probably the last sharp take-off with an Me 163 in Husum was made by Hauptmann Herbert Frömert on 27 April 1945, a few days after Hauptmann Rudi Opitz, *Gruppenkommandeur* II./JG 400, made his last 'sharp' start;

'The pilots from the other *Staffeln*, including Hauptmann Opitz, joined us at Husum at the end of April. They had had to leave their aircraft behind at Wittmundhafen and Jever. Opitz wished to fly the Me 163 once more and for this purpose was allocated an aircraft from my *Staffel* [7./JG 400], one which had successfully completed an engine ground test only that morning [25 April]. The aircraft took off normally but during the climb started emitting a trail of smoke from below the fuselage. We told him what was happening. We were never to learn exactly why Rudolf Opitz did not reply or why he did not immediately bale out of his burning aircraft.

'He broke off his flight at a height of about 3,000-4,000 metres and dived back to the airfield. There was still time for him to have baled out. Flames as well as the smoke were by then visible. He flew a circuit around the airfield to kill his speed and then flew away from the airfield to turn prior to landing. During the last part of the turn the Me 163 appeared to become uncontrollable and the next thing we saw was a pall of smoke rising from behind a small hill. Nobody thought he could have survived the accident but we found him lying in a ditch not far from the burning wreckage. It was apparent that he

Husum: Leutnant Reinhard Opitz, *Staffelkapitän* 7./JG 400, assists Hauptmann Rudolf Opitz, *Gruppenkommandeur* II./JG 400, during preparations for take-off. Hauptmann Opitz made the last sharp take-off from Husum on 25 April shortly before the end of the war in Europe. His flight ended in a crash landing after the engine caught fire (*Reinhard Opitz*)

had managed to release the canopy and his seat harness and that the belly landing had thrown him out of the cockpit. He was nursed back to health in a hospital in Husum and we took him, under somewhat adventurous circumstances, in a lorry to Augsburg at the end of July. An investigation of the wreckage revealed that he could not bale out because his parachute had been burnt by leaking *T-Stoff*.'

Reinhard Opitz;

'The ceasefire came into effect at 8 o'clock in the morning on 8 May 1945. A large number of aircraft had taken off at dawn with the object of reaching other airfields or places close to where the pilots lived. A Ju 88 from the weather reconnaissance squadron had returned from a flight over the North Sea two hours earlier and brought with it for the last time the latest weather report. The British Army had reached the Nordostseekanal that morning and, at the end of the war, we were still free.

'Two days later the Duty Officer reported to the *Horstkommandant* during lunch in the mess that a British armoured reconnaissance vehicle was parked in front of the gate and was asking permission to enter! The formal surrender of the airfield, together with our *Gruppe*, other fighter squadrons and a part of a *Staffel* of Heinkel He 162 *Volksjäger*, followed soon afterwards.

'During the next few days we had to ward off wandering and armed Russian soldiers. A little later, a Lancaster bomber bearing battle scars from night-time raids over Germany brought with it a group of

British officers who expressed an interest in the Me 163. As we had received orders from Dönitz's government not to destroy any aircraft or equipment and to await further instructions, approximately 14 combat ready Me 163s and 12 or 15 disassembled Me 163s fell into the hands of the British. All troops, including flying personnel, had, in the meantime, been transferred to a large fenced-off area some 20km from Husum.'

Peter Gerth recalled;

'I made two demonstration flights of the Me 163 for the British. I was brought to Husum from a PoW camp at Eiderstedt for this purpose. Later, I was to accompany maintenance personnel to London but nothing came of this plan.'

Reinhard Opitz 'was commandeered with 20 men from our *Staffel* to pack a number of these aircraft together with spare parts in large containers according to our captors' instructions. Discussions with the British officers and engineers were conducted correctly, even in a friendly fashion.

'A part of the airfield was used to park thousands of German army vehicles and the empty hangars were used to store large quantities of valuable instruments, parachutes and other aircraft equipment. We could even inspect famous British fighter squadrons at close quarters as the airfield was, for a time, the base of Spitfire 21s and Tempests. Nobody prevented us from looking at these aircraft and if there were any difficulties we simply had to show our passes issued by the British commander.'

Me 163B Wk-Nr. 190598, photographed at Husum after the surrender of the airfield (*EN Archive*)

APPENDICES

APPENDIX 1

UNIT ORGANISATION AND PERSONNEL

Command Organisation

JG 400

Geschwaderkommodore Major Wolfgang Späte, RK, EL, DK
(November 1944 - April 1945)

I./JG 400

Formed Brandis, August 1944. Dispersed Brandis, April 1945.
Gruppenkommandeur Major Wolfgang Späte, RK, EL, DK
(August - October 1944)
Acting *Gruppenkommandeur* Hauptmann Rudolf Opitz, EK I
(October - November 1944)
Gruppenkommandeur Hauptmann Wilhelm Fulda, RK
(December 1944 - February 1945)
Gruppenkommandeur Hauptmann Albert Falderbaum
(February - April 1945)

1./JG 400

Formed Wittmundhafen as 20./JG 1, February 1944.
Transferred to Brandis, July 1944. Dispersed Brandis,
April 1945.
Staffelkapitän Hauptmann Robert Olejnik, RK (March - April
1944)
Staffelführer Hauptmann Otto Böhner (April - May 1944)
Staffelkapitän Oberleutnant Rudolf Opitz, EK I (May - July
1944)
Staffelkapitän Hauptmann Robert Olejnik, RK, EP (August -
November 1944)
Staffelführer Hauptmann Albert Falderbaum (December 1944
- February 1945)
Staffelkapitän Hauptmann Albert Falderbaum (February 1945)

2./JG 400

Formed Oranienburg, March 1944. Transferred to Venlo, July
1944; to Brandis, September 1944. Dispersed Brandis, April
1945.
Staffelkapitän Hauptmann Otto Böhner, EK I, EK II (July 1944
- February 1945)
Staffelführer Hauptmann Johannes Polzin (February - April
1945)

3./JG 400

In process of being established at Brandis as 3./JG 400 in
August 1944 but renumbered 5./JG 400 in November
1944.

New *Staffel*, 3./JG 400, established at Brandis in November
1944. Dispersed Brandis, April 1945.
Staffelführer Oberleutnant Franz Rösle (November 1944 -
February 1945)
Staffelkapitän Oberleutnant Franz Rösle (February - April
1945)

4./JG 400

In process of formation at Brandis in August 1944 and order
for its establishment was issued in September but this
order was rescinded in November 1944
Staffelführer Hauptmann Heinrich Sturm (September -
November 1944)

II./JG 400

Formed Brandis, August 1944. Transferred to Stargard,
November 1944; to Jever (*Stab* only), February 1945; to
Husum (*Stab* only), April 1945. Surrendered Husum,
May 1945.
Gruppenkommandeur Hauptmann Rudolf Opitz, EK I
(November 1944 - May 1945)

5./JG 400

Originally formed at Brandis as 3./JG 400 in August 1944.
Renumbered 5./JG 400 in November 1944. Transferred
to Stargard, October 1944; to Bad Zwischenahn via
Stendal, January 1945. Surrendered Bad Zwischenahn,
April 1945.
Staffelführer Hauptmann Jochen Langen (September -
October 1944)
Staffelführer/Staffelkapitän Oberleutnant Franz Woidich,
RK, DK (October 1944 - April 1945)

6./JG 400

Originally formed at Brandis as 4./JG 400 in August 1944. Renumbered 6./JG 400 in November 1944. Transferred to Stargard, October 1944; to Wittmundhafen, via Salzwedel, January 1945. Surrendered Wittmundhafen, April 1945.

Staffelführer Oberleutnant Franz Woidich, RK, DK (September - October 1944)

Staffelführer/Staffelkapitän Leutnant Peter Gerth (October 1944 - April 1945)

7./JG 400

Formed Stettin-Altdam, November 1944. Transferred to Salzwedel, February 1945; to Nordholz, March 1945; to Husum, April 1945. Surrendered Husum, May 1945.

Staffelführer/Staffelkapitän Leutnant Reinhard Opitz, EK (October 1944 – May 1945)

Erg.St./JG 400

Formed Bad Zwischenahn, July 1944. Transferred to Brandis, July 1944; to Udetfeld, October 1944. Incorporated in IV./EJG 2 and renumbered 13./EJG 2, November 1944.

Staffelführer Leutnant Franz Medicus (July - August 1944)

Staffelkapitän Hauptmann Hans Nocher (September - October 1944)

IV./EJG 2

Formed Brandis, November 1944. Transferred to Sprottau, December 1944; to Esperstedt, February 1945; to Schleswig-Holstein, March 1945.

Gruppenkommandeur Hauptmann Robert Olejnik, RK (December 1944 - March 1945)

13./EJG 2

Formerly *Erg.St./*JG 400. At Udetfeld, October - January 1945. Transferred to Esperstedt, February 1945; to Brandis, February 1945.

Staffelkapitän Oberleutnant Adolf Niemeyer (November 1944 - March 1945)

14./EJG 2

Formed Brandis, November 1944. Transferred to Sprottau, December 1944; to Esperstedt, February 1945; to Brandis, February 1945.

Staffelkapitän Leutnant Hermann Ziegler (November 1944 - March 1945)

15./EJG 2

Formed Brandis, November 1944. Transferred to Sprottau, December 1944; to Esperstedt, February 1945.

Staffelkapitän Hauptmann Erwin Sturm (November 1944 - January 1945)

APPENDIX 2

PILOTS SERVING WITH JG 400, Erg.St/JG 400 AND IV./EJG 2

Maj. Gerhard Fichtner	5./JG 400	Oblt. Hans Könnecke	6./JG 400
		Oblt. Herbert Leiterer	?./JG 400
Hptm. Herbert Frömert	II./JG 400	Oblt. Kurt Müller, EK I, EK II	I./JG 400
Hptm. Jürgen Hepe	I./JG 400	Oblt. Schulz	1./JG 400 (Killed in accident, 13.9.44)
Hptm. Ehrenfried Schulze	1./JG 400		
Hptm. Bernhard Graf von Schweinitz	1./JG 400; 2./JG 400	Oblt. Wolfgang Wollenweber	13./EJG 2
Oblt. Dietrich Angermann	Erg.St./JG 400	Lt. Günter Andreas	2./JG 400
Oblt. Wolfgang Baudis	Erg.St./JG 400; 1./JG 400	Lt. Erwin Bauer	Erg.St./JG 400
		Lt. Hans Bott, EK II	1./JG 400 (Wounded in action, 11.10.44)
Oblt. Joachim Bialucha	2./JG 400 (Killed in accident, 12.8.44)		
		Lt. Paul Braun	1./JG 400
Oblt. Heinz Dönnicke	1./JG 400 (Killed in accident, 13.1.45)	Lt. von Donner	?./JG 400
		Lt. Albrecht Finke	?./JG 400
Oblt. Gerhard Eberle	1./JG 400; 5./JG 400	Lt. Siegfried Graf	I./JG 400
Oblt. Hans-Werner Ertel	4./JG 400	Lt. Egon Grosse	4./JG 400
Oblt. Hans Fasel	4./JG 400	Lt. Walter Haselin	Erg.St./JG 400
Oblt. Fritz-Joachim Grohmann	2./JG 400	Lt. Herbert Hoffer-Sulmthal	?./JG 400
Oblt. Ludwig Köhl	1./JG 400	Lt. Werner Jung	14./EJG 2

Lt. Friedrich Kelb	2./JG 400
Lt. Kurt Kraft	?./JG 400
Lt. Werner Lehn	6./JG 400
Lt. Hans-Ludwig Löscher	14./EJG 2; 1./JG 400
Lt. Hartmut Ryll	1./JG 400 (Killed in combat, 16.8.44)
Lt. Rolf Schlegel	2./JG 400
Lt. Heinz Schubert	2./JG 400
Ofw. Jakob Bollenrath	2./JG 400 (Killed in combat, 2.11.44)
Ofw. Friedrich-Peter Husser, EK I	1./JG 400; 2./JG 400 (Wounded in action, 7.10.44)
Ofw. Otto Krutsch	1./JG 400
Ofw. Kristoph Kurz	2./JG 400
Ofw. Wilhelm Josef Mühlstroh	1./JG 400
Ofw. August Müller	1./JG 400
Ofw. Werner Nelte	1./JG 400 (Killed in combat, 14.4.45)
Ofw. Helmut Reukauf	1./JG 400 (Killed in accident, 13.9.44)
Ofw. Horst Rolly	2./JG 400 (Killed in accident, 2.11.44)
Ofw. Herbert Straznicky	1./JG 400 (Killed in combat, 2.11.44)
Ofhr. Breuker	II./JG 400
Fw. Fleischmann	?./JG 400 (Killed in accident, 15.3.45)
Fw. Rolf Glogner, EK I, EK II	2./JG 400
Fw. Detlef Hamburger	?/JG 400
Fw. Gottfried Hauss	Erg.St./JG 400; 13./EJG 2
Fw. Herbert Klein	14./EJG 2; 1./JG 400
Fw. Gerhard Mohr	1./JG 400
Fw. Ingo Päsold	I./JG 400
Fw. Schametz	2./JG 400
Fw. Ernst Schelper	2./JG 400
Fw. Kurt Schiebeler, EK II	1./JG 400
Fw. Schorries	13./EJG 2
Fw. Siegfried Schubert	1./JG 400 (Killed in accident, 7.10.44)
Fw. Waldemar Wallaschofski	?./JG 400
Fw. Hans Wiedemann	1./JG 400 (Killed in combat, 13.4.45)
Fw. Ernst Zielsdorf	2./JG 400
Fw. Rudolf Zimmermann	1./JG 400
Fhr. Carl Marsen (Magersuppe)	I./JG 400

Uffz. Manfred Eisenmann	2./JG 400 (Killed in accident, 7.10.44)
Uffz. Rolf Ernst	1./JG 400
Uffz. Ferner	2./JG 400
Uffz. Siegfried Graf	I./JG 400
Uffz. Herbert Hentschel	2./JG 400
Uffz. Werner Husemann	?./JG 400
Uffz. Egon Kerckhoff	?./JG 400
Uffz. Kurt Konrad	?./JG 400
Uffz. Karl Maurer	?./JG 400
Uffz. Josef Mentenich	2./JG 400
Uffz. Georg Neher	2./JG 400
Uffz. Ferdinand Schmitz	?./JG 400
Uffz. Oswin Schüller	1./JG 400
Uffz. Ludwig Schweiger	?./JG 400 (Reported missing, 1945)
Uffz. Udo Schwenger	?./JG 400
Uffz. Slaby	?./JG 400
Uffz. Siegfried? Sommer	?/JG 400
Uffz. Heribert Sponheuer	?
Uffz. Anton Steidl	1./JG 400
Uffz. Steinmetz	I./JG 400
Uffz. Anton Süss	2./JG 400
Uffz. Thomas	2./JG 400
Uffz. Weichold	Erg.St./JG 400; IV./EJG 2
Uffz. Leo Zielonka	?./JG 400
Ogefr. Bernd von Bremen	3./JG 400
Ogefr. Hans Dehramann	?./JG 400 (Killed in accident, 21.1.45)
Ogefr. Hermann Giesel	13./EJG 2 (Killed in combat, 17.12.44)
Ogefr. Franz Kalt	2./JG 400
Ogefr. Horst Lachmann	Erg.St./JG 400; 14./EJG 2; 3./JG 400
Ogefr. Gerhard Stolle	14./EJG 2; 2./JG 400
Flg. (Hptm.) Walter Dittmar	I./JG 400

APPENDIX 3

BIOGRAPHIES

Hauptmann Otto Böhner

Born 14 December 1913, Hamburg. 1934-35, studied engineering and in same period gained first of his pilots' licences. Enlisted in Luftwaffe at Oldenburg where he gained B licence. Obtained C licence at *Flugzeugführerschule*, Ludwigslust, in October 1937. Afterwards joined fighter school at Werneuchen. April 1937, transferred as Leutnant to 4./JG 334 (later renamed JG 53) at Mannheim. Served in French campaign; claimed three aircraft destroyed. Shot down on 10 June 1940; injured while baling out and taken prisoner by the French. At end of French campaign, released and sent to Bordeaux, returning from there to Mannheim via Paris. Sent to Luftwaffe hospital at Wismar to recover from injuries. Reported back to JG 53 at Dinan, Brittany, but shortly afterwards was transferred as staff officer to flying school in Silesia. October 1940, appointed *Staffelkapitän*, 6./JG 53. Flew escort fighter duties during Battle of Britain; claimed two aircraft destroyed. From October 1940 to September 1941, served with squadron at Berck-sur-mer, St Omer, Jever, Berlin-Döberitz, Westerland and Bergen von See (The Netherlands). December 1941, transferred to Sicily via Munich and Foggia. During the Battle of Malta aircraft damaged by anti-aircraft fire over Malta but he managed to return to base. After March 1942 served as technical officer with JG 53 in North Africa. Joined *Erprobungskommando* (EKdo) 16 at Peenemünde in August 1943, shortly before transfer of unit to Bad Zwischenahn. January 1944, became technical officer, EKdo 16, after death of Oberleutnant Josef 'Joschi' Pöhs. Appointed *Staffelführer* 1./JG 400 at Wittmundhafen after accident to Olejnik on 21 April. Joined 2./JG 400 at Venlo in July as *Staffelkapitän*, after convalescence from own accident at Wittmundhafen on May 28. Transferred to Brandis with squadron at beginning of September 1944. Ordered to join German Army at Eger (Cheb), Czechoslovakia, April 1945.

Flugkapitän Heinrich 'Heini' Dittmar

Born 30 March 1911, Bad Kissingen. Attended Handelsschule, Schweinfurt. 1925-29, successful participant in various German model aircraft competitions. 1929, joined *Rhön-Rossitten-Gesellschaft* (RRG) at Wasserkuppe where he gained A and B gliding licences. 1931-32, designed and constructed Condor series of gliders. Won 1932 and 1933 Rhön competitions. Accompanied Georgii on expedition to South America where he established world altitude record (4,675m) for gliders in February 1934. World distance record (375km) for gliders with flight to Liban, Czechoslovakia, achieved during 1934 Rhön competition. Established world altitude record (2,700 metres) for two-seater gliders in 1934. Achieved first crossing of the Alps with glider in 1935. Won first international Alpine gliding competition held in 1937 at Jungfraujoch. 1937, became world champion at first international gliding championship held at Wasserkuppe and was awarded Hindenburg Trophy for Gliding Flight. 1938, awarded Gold Medal for Gliding Flight by ISTUS. 1938, NSFK-Hauptstürmführer. In 1936 became test pilot with *Deutsches Forschungsinstitut für Segelflug* (DFS), Darmstadt, (name changed to *Deutsche Forschungsanstalt für Segelflug* (DFS) in 1937) and, in 1939, with Department L, Messerschmitt AG, Augsburg. Conducted first flights of DFS 194 and Me 163A. During flight testing of Me 163A V4 in 1941 became first pilot to exceed speed of 1,000km/h, for which he was promoted to rank of Flugkapitän and awarded Lilienthal Prize for Aviation Research. 1942, badly injured during flight testing of Me 163. After war returned to industry. Recommenced designing and building gliders in 1951 after removal of Allies' restrictions on gliding. Killed in gliding accident on 28 April 1960 at Mühlheim on the river Ruhr.

Hauptmann Albert Falderbaum

Born 10 April 1913, Niederpleis, near Bonn. Started flying at age of 17, making first solo flight in a powered aircraft one year later. 1931, gained licence for aerobatics in powered aircraft. Joined Luftwaffe as flying instructor in 1934. Participated for first time in German aerobatic championships in 1937 (achieved second position). In 1938 and 1939 became German aerobatic champion. From outbreak of war to August 1943 served as flying instructor with instructor training school, Brandenburg-Briest. Promoted to Leutnant, July 1941, Oberleutnant, July 1942, and Hauptmann, July 1943. August-October 1943, instructor with *Blindflugschule* 10, Altenburg. October 1943-August 1944, *Gruppenkommandeur*, I./JG 110. August-October 1944, *Frontflieger-Sammelstelle*, Quedlinburg. October-November 1944, converted to Me 163 with *Ergänzungsstaffel*/JG 400 at Brandis. Joined 1./JG 400 in December 1944, succeeding Hauptmann Robert Olejnik as *Staffelkapitän* of 1./JG 400, who became *Gruppenkommandeur* of IV./EJG 2, and Hauptmann Wilhelm Fulda as *Gruppenkommandeur* of I./JG 400 in February 1945. After the war, sales manager for Shell AG; also participated in competitions outside Germany until 1955, when he again took part in national events. Killed during test flight of SIAT-222 on 29 September 1961, Augsburg (his parachute became entangled with the aircraft while attempting to bale out).

Hauptmann Wilhelm Fulda

Born 21 May 1909, Antwerp, Belgium. As Leutnant, awarded *Ritterkreuz* on 14 June 1941 for action as commander of transport glider group during attack on Corinthian Isthmus, Greece. Served with: 3./LLG 1, August-December 1941; 17./KGzbV 1, December 1941-February 1942; 1. *Gotha-Staffel*/KGrzbV 1, February-June 1942; as staff officer, 1./LLG 2, June-December 1942; *Ergänzungsgruppe* (S) 1, December 1942-August 1943; as technical officer, *Stab*/JG 301, August-November 1943; as *Staffelkapitän*, 9./JG 301, November 1943-January 1944; as *Gruppenkommandeur*, II./JG 301, January-February 1944; *Sichtungsstelle des Generals der Jagdflieger*, February-July 1944; as *Kommodore der Ergänzungsjagdgruppe*, August 1944; II./JG 4, August-September 1944; as *Gruppenkommandeur*, I./JG 302, October 1944; as *Gruppenkommandeur*, I./JG 400, January-February 1945. He led the remnants of I./JG 400 who served as infantry in the area between Eger and Schirnding, April-May 1945. Died in Hamburg on 8 August 1977.

Leutnant Peter Gerth

Born 5 July 1921, Pforzheim, Baden-Wüttemberg. Fighter pilot instructor with 3. and 4. *Staffel*, JFS 5, July 1941-September 1943. Promoted to Leutnant, June 1942. Afterwards with II./JG 51. Fighter pilot instructor, 1./*Jagdgruppe-Ost*, January-March 1944. With EKdo 16, March-October 1944. *Staffelführer*/*Staffelkapitän*, 6./JG 400, November 1944-April 1945.

Dr.phil.nat. Alexander Martin Lippisch

Born 1 November 1894, Munich. Interest in aeronautics inspired by Orville Wright's flights at Tempelhof, Berlin, in September 1909. Conscripted in the German Army at the outbreak of war and served as aerial reconnaissance photographic interpreter and cartographer on the Eastern Front. On cessation of hostilities on this front in December 1917, posted as assistant aerodynamicist to Zeppelin Works, Lindau-Reutin, but referred to Claude Dornier at Seemoos, near Friedrichshafen on Lake Constance. At the end of war he was with Dornier at Zech near Lindau. Left Dornier in December 1918. Afterwards set up organisation and secured contract from Brazilian Government to produce maps of Brazil from aerial photographs but was forced to cancel contract under terms of Versailles Treaty. Joined Fritz Schweizer at Wasserkuppe as aerodynamicist in 1921. There also assisted Espenlaub with design of tailless glider. Remained at Wasserkuppe where he joined Weltensegler GmbH in autumn of 1922, for whom he designed a number of gliders. November 1923 joined Steinmann-Flugzeugbau at Hagen, Westphalia, where he started developing tailless, swept-winged gliders (flight tests conducted at nearby

Winterberg). 1925, appointed head of Technical Department of RRG Research Institute, Wasserkuppe, under Georgii, producing the Storch and Delta series of gliders, motor-gliders and light aircraft. 1928 conducted series of tests with rocket-propelled models with his brother-in-law, Fritz Stamer, prior to trials with rocket-propelled Ente under contract to Opel. 1934, retained by DFS Darmstadt; continued to develop Delta and other designs. 1936 began work on DFS 194, forerunner of Me 163. Joined Messerschmitt AG on 2 January 1939 to develop Me 163, there becoming head of Department L. Received doctorate from Heidelberg University on 29 March 1943 for thesis, 'Flugmechanische Beziehungen des Fluges mit Strahlenantrieb (Flight mechanics of jet-propelled flight)'. Left Messerschmitt AG on 28 April 1943, taking up appointment on 1 May as head of the *Luftfahrtforschungsanstalt* Vienna; retained as consultant with Messerschmitt for further development of Me 163. In Vienna produced designs for Lorin-engined and ram-jet powered delta-winged aircraft. Fled Vienna on approach of Soviet troops, eventually reaching Strobl on Wolfgangsee. There discovered by US troops. Interrogated by Allies in Paris on 23 May 1945. Transferred to Wimbledon, London, for further interrogation. After January 1946 employed as consultant aerodynamicist by USAAF Air Technical Command, Wright Field, Dayton, Ohio, and in 1947 by the US Navy Air Material Center Philadelphia. 1949 joined Collins Radio Corporation, developing remotely piloted aircraft (drones) and aerodyne concept. In February 1950 became head of Collins' Fluid Dynamics Research Group at Cedar Rapids, Iowa, and led development of surface skimmers based on wing-in-ground-effect (WIG) principle. In 1966 founded Lippisch Research Corporation to further development of WIG designs, which were also built by Rhein-Flugzeugbau and flight tested by Späte on Lake Constance. 1972, consultant to Dornier on development of drones employing aerodyne concept. Lippisch died in Cedar Rapids on 11 February 1976.

Oberleutnant Franz Medicus

Born 3 June 1909, Bobingen, near Augsburg. 1928, gained A and B licences, at gliding school, Wangen/Allgau and, in 1930, C licence at Hesselberg, near Gerolsfingen, Bavaria. After 1934 he was a gliding instructor. Gained powered aircraft licence in 1935. 1937-39, head of gliding school at Hesselberg. Attended flying courses organised by *Luftgaureserve* and qualified for BI and BII powered aircraft licences. Completed flying instructor course at Brandenburg-Briest in 1940 and afterwards taught at Kaufbeuren and Gelnhausen. Served with JG 104, October 1943-February 1944. Joined EKdo 16, Bad Zwischenahn, February 1944. Appointed *Staffelführer*,

Ergänzungsstaffel/JG 400, Brandis, July 1944. Served with 6./JG 400, October 1944-February 1945 and 5./JG 400, February-May 1945. After war, test pilot with Scheibe. In 1954, honorary gliding consultant, *Luftsport-Verband Bayern eV*. Killed in flying accident at Unterwössen, Chiemgau, on 27 October 1960.

Oberleutnant Adolf Niemeyer

Born 17 April 1912, Hameln. Served with: *Segelflugzeug-ausbildungsstelle der Luftwaffe* July 1943-April 1944; EKdo 16, April-August 1944; *Ergänzungsstaffel*/JG 400, August-November 1944; as *Staffelkapitän*, 13./EJG 2, November 1944-March 1945; JG 400, March-April 1945. Died in Hameln, 2002. Up to his death he was the oldest person in Germany holding a pilot's licence and flying helicopters!

Hauptmann Robert Ignatz Olejnik

Born 9 March 1911 in Borbeck (now a suburb of Essen). Joined DVS in October 1933 and Luftwaffe in March 1935. Joined 2./JG 3 as Oberfeldwebel in 1936. Participated in Battle of Britain (5 victories). Awarded EK II on 9 September and EK I on 30 September 1940. As Leutnant, took command of 1./JG 3 (later renamed 4./JG 1), becoming *Staffelkapitän* of that unit in May 1941. Received *Ehrenpokal* from Reichsmarschall Göring on 18 July 1941. Awarded *Ritterkreuz* as Oberleutnant on 30 July 1941 (41 victories). Autumn 1941, transferred with squadron to Holland; at that time had claimed 37 victories. Served with 4./JG 1 until May 1943, when he temporarily took over command of II./JG 1. In July 1943 promoted to *Gruppenkommandeur*, III./JG 1. Joined EKdo 16, October 1943. Appointed *Staffelkapitän*, 1./JG 400, Wittmundhafen, March 1944. Returned to duty at Brandis mid-July after recovery from take-off accident with Me 163B V16 at Wittmundhafen on April 21. Resumed command of 1./JG 400 in September 1944. In December 1944 became *Gruppenkommandeur*, IV./EJG 2, based at Sprottau. End January 1945, transferred with IV. *Gruppe* to Esperstedt where it remained till mid-April (some of group's pilots transferred to JG 400 at Brandis in February). Olejnik returned to Brandis shortly before evacuation of airfield in April and joined army unit ordered to move south through Dresden to Eger (Cheb), Czechoslovakia, where he was taken prisoner by American forces. He ended war credited with 42 victories. He died in Munich on 29 October 1988.

Leutnant Reinhard Opitz

Born 17 August 1923, Rüdesheim am Rhein. Gained first gliding licence in 1938. Joined Luftwaffe 1941 as officer cadet. 1942, trained as pilot at *Luftkriegsschule* II, Berlin-Gatow. 1943, fighter pilot training, *Zerstörerschule* II,

Neubiberg. Promoted to Leutnant, June 1943. With ZG 101 until August 1944 as operational pilot and fighter pilot instructor; claimed two aircraft destroyed (B-17 and P-51); Opitz himself shot down February 1944. Transferred to *Ergänzungsstaffel*/JG 400 at Brandis, August 1944, becoming *Staffelführer* 7./JG 400 at Stettin-Altdamm in November 1944, and *Staffelkapitän* 7./JG 400 in February 1945. Transferred with squadron to Husum via Salzwedel and Nordholz, February 1945. Helped to dismantle Me 163s at Husum at end of war. Became prisoner of war June 1945; released 1946, thereafter employed in engineering industry. 1951, gained degree (Dipl.-Ing.) in metallurgical engineering and was awarded doctorate (Dr.-Ing.E.h.) in 1985. Renewed gliding licence in 1952 and private pilot's licence in 1956.

Hauptmann Paul Rudolf 'Rudi' Opitz

Born 9 August 1910, Landeshut, Silesia (today Kamienna Góra, Poland). 1927-1934, trained and employed as joiner and cabinet maker, specialising in wooden aircraft construction. 1935-1939, gliding instructor with *Rhön-Rossitten-Gesellschaft* (RRG), Wasserkuppe, and *Reichs-Schlepp- und Kunstflugschule*, Darmstadt-Griesheim, and instructor and test pilot with *Institut für Segelflug* and *Institut für Flugversuche*, DFS Darmstadt. Obtained B1 and C licences. In 1935, 1936 and 1938 participant in various gliding competitions. Awarded gold medal by ISTUS, silver medal by NSFK and silver medal by the city of Darmstadt for his gliding achievements. September 1939 enlisted as Flieger in Luftwaffe; served with *Sturmabteilung Koch* with which he participated in the attack with DFS 230 assault gliders on Fort Eben Emael and bridges over the Albert Canal, Dutch-Belgian border, on 10 May 1940; awarded EK I and promoted to Feldwebel. Assigned to Gliding School Hildesheim to help train pilots for this form of warfare, eventually taking charge of all airfields under *Fliegerschule für Lastensegler* 4. In May 1941, transferred to Frankfurt am Main. Promoted to Leutnant. August 1941, joined Department L, Messerschmitt AG, and posted as test pilot to Peenemünde. May 1942, joined EKdo 16 at Peenemünde and transferred with unit to Bad Zwischenahn. May 1944, replaced Hauptmann Otto Böhner as *Staffelkapitän*, 1./JG 400, after Hauptmann Otto Böhner's accident at Wittmundhafen, and transferred with squadron to Brandis in July 1944. Appointed *Gruppenkommandeur*, I./JG 400, in October and *Gruppenkommandeur*, II./JG 400, in November 1944, transferring with latter unit from Brandis to Stargard and then to Husum. On 8 May 1945, surrendered II./JG 400 then at Husum to RAF Regiment. After war employed by USAAF Air Technical Command, Wright Field, Dayton, Ohio, and later as supervisor, gas turbine flight test operations,

Avco-Lycoming, Stratford, Connecticut. 'Rudi' Opitz died in the USA on 1 May 2010.

Oberleutnant Franz Rösle

Born 20 March 1920 in Augsburg. Served with 1./JG 400 at Wittmundhafen and Brandis, March-September 1944; Staffelkapitän, 3./JG 400, Brandis, November 1944-April 1945.

Major Wolfgang Späte

Born 8 September 1911, Dresden. 1927 obtained gliding licences, Wasserkuppe. After 1934, participant in various national and international gliding competitions. Overall winner of 1938 Rhön competition. Holder of Goldenes Leistungsabzeichen für Segelflug No. 7. In 1937 became test pilot with DFS Darmstadt and started studies in engineering at TH Darmstadt. At outbreak of war enlisted as Leutnant der Reserve and served in Polish and French campaigns with Army Reconnaissance Squadron 2./H23, flying Hs 126. On 1 January 1941, transferred to 5./JG 54 as fighter pilot; flew Bf 109 in Balkans and on Eastern Front. On 9 August 1941, awarded Ehrenpokal by Reichsmarschall Göring. September 1941 promoted to Staffelkapitän, 5./JG 54. As Oberleutnant awarded Ritterkreuz on 5 October 1941 (45 victories) and on 20 December 1941, Deutsches Kreuz. On 23 April 1942 awarded Eichenlaub to Ritterkreuz (72 victories). May 1942, promoted to Hauptmann and nominated Typenbegleiter Me 163 and commander of EKdo 16 responsible for its operational development trials. May 1944, Gruppenkommandeur, IV./JG 54; served on Eastern and Western Fronts. August 1944, Gruppenkommandeur, I./JG 400, Brandis. Promoted to Major. December 1944, Geschwaderkommodore, JG 400. April 1945, posted as Gruppenkommandeur to I./JG 7 (Me 262) at Alt-Lönnewitz, afterwards transferring with unit to Prague. Ended war credited with 99 victories. After war, test pilot for French Air Force and, later, director, photographic company, Frankfurt am Main. 1956-67, served as Oberstleutnant with West German Air Force. 1967-71, worked with Alexander Lippisch and flight tested his surface skimming aircraft. In retirement worked as aviation journalist. Späte died at Edewicht, near Oldenburg, on 30 April 1997.

Oberleutnant Franz Woidich

Born 2 January 1921, Znaim, Bohemia (today, Znojmo, Czech Republic). Joined 5./JG 27 in July 1941 as Oberfähnrich; served in North Africa (credited with two victories). April 1942, transferred to 3./JG 52 on the Eastern Front; June 1943 promoted to Staffelkapitän. Received Ehrenpokal from Reichsmarschall Göring on 13 September 1943 and awarded Deutsches Kreuz on 6 December 1943. At end of 1943 credited with 56 victories. Became Staffelkapitän,

5. (Sturm)/JG 4, May 1944. As Leutnant awarded Ritterkreuz on 9 June 1944 (80 victories). Commenced training on Me 163 with Ergänzungsstaffel/JG 400 on 11 August 1944. Joined 4./JG 400 at Brandis on 11 September (this squadron was subsequently renumbered 6./JG 400). Promoted to Oberleutnant. Served as Staffelführer/Staffelkapitän 5./JG 400, November 1944-April 1945. Ended war credited with 110 victories (107 claimed on Eastern Front).

Leutnant Hermann 'Mano' Ziegler

Born 7 June 1908, Wyhlen, near Lörrach. 1928 entered College for Physical Education, Berlin, afterwards achieving personal success in high-diving and selection as member of German Olympic core team. Became student world diving champion in 1932 and 1934. Orphaned, he took up writing to finance studies and to support himself. 1932-39, assistant to head of Publicity Department, Auto-Union. At outbreak of war enlisted in the Luftwaffe, rising to rank of Leutnant. Volunteered for service with EKdo 16, joining that unit at Bad Zwischenahn in October 1943. Seconded to Jesau as technical officer in June to assist with flight testing Me 163s completed by Klemm. Returned to Bad Zwischenahn July 1944 and transferred to Ergänzungsstaffel/JG 400 at Brandis in September. November 1944, promoted to Staffelkapitän 14./EJG 2 and served at Rangsdorf, Sprottau and Esperstedt before returning to Brandis in February 1945. Held prisoner by Soviet Army on return to Berlin after the war but managed to escape to the West. In the late 1940s and early 1950s earned living as artist, actor, cabaret artist, reporter, author and car salesman. 1957-62, journalist and chief editor, Flug Revue. Afterwards head of Publicity Departments of Heinkel (1962-64), Messerschmitt (1965-69) and Deutsche Airbus (1969-71). Ziegler died in Isny, Germany, October 1991.

OPERATIONAL FLIGHT LOG

Me 163	Werk-nummer	Call sign	Other marking	Date	Place	Unit	Pilot	Flight mode	Remarks
I./JG 400									
BV29	16310038	GH+IH	—	16.05.44	Wittmundhafen	1./JG 400	Voy (Klemm)	TG	Made four flights same day
		GH+IH	—	18.05.44	Wittmundhafen	1./JG 400	Voy (Klemm)	TG	Made two flights same day
		GH+IH	—	22.05.44	Wittmundhafen	1./JG 400	Voy (Klemm)	C	
		GH+IH	—	11.06.44	Wittmundhafen → Rechlin-Lärz	1./JG 400	Schiebeler	TG	Transfer flight
		GH+IH	—	12.06.44-13.06.44	Rechlin-Lärz	1./JG 400	Opitz, Rudolf	C	RLM demonstration (Göring, Milch, Italian and Japanese delegations). Participated in formation take-off with BV54 and one other unidentified Me 163. Solo flight by Opitz; aircraft damaged on landing; Opitz injured; Schiebeler helped in rescue
BV31	16310040	GH+IJ	—	19.08.44	Brandis	?./JG 400	Opitz, Reinhard	TG	
		GH+IJ	—	20.08.44	Brandis	?./JG 400	Opitz, Reinhard	TG	
		GH+IJ	—	22.08.44	Brandis	?./JG 400	Opitz, Reinhard	TG	Made two flights same day
		GH+IJ	—	02.10.44	Brandis	?./JG 400	Krutsch	TG	
BV43	16310052	PK+QN	—	18.04.44	Wittmundhafen	1./JG 400	Voy (Klemm)	TG	
		PK+QN	—	19.04.44	Wittmundhafen	1./JG 400	Voy (Klemm)	C	
		PK+QN	—	29.04.44	Wittmundhafen	1./JG 400	Voy (Klemm)	TG	
		PK+QN	—	04.05.44	Wittmundhafen	1./JG 400	Voy (Klemm)	TG	
		PK+QN	—	10.05.44	Wittmundhafen	1./JG 400	Voy (Klemm)	TG	Made two flights same day
		PK+QN	—	12.05.44	Wittmundhafen	1./JG 400	Voy (Klemm)	TG	Made two flights same day
		PK+QN	—	13.05.44	Wittmundhafen	1./JG 400	Voy (Klemm)	C	
		PK+QN	—	22.05.44	Wittmundhafen	1./JG 400	Zimmermann	TG	
BV44	16310053	PK+QO	—	19.06.44	Wittmundhafen	1./JG 400	Schiebeler	C	
		PK+QO	—	29.06.44	Wittmundhafen	1./JG 400	Schiebeler	C	
BV46	16310055	PK+QQ	—	19.05.44	Wittmundhafen	1./JG 400	Voy (Klemm)	TG + C	Made four flights same day (1st, 3rd, 4th TG; 2nd C)
		PK+QQ	—	22.05.44	Wittmundhafen	1./JG 400	Voy (Klemm)	C	
BV48	16310057	PK+QS	—	24.05.44	Wittmundhafen	1./JG 400	Voy (Klemm)	TG + C	Made three flights same day (1st, 3rd TG; 2nd C)
		PK+QS	—	19.06.44	Wittmundhafen	1./JG 400	Schiebeler	C	
		PK+QS	—	??.07.44	Wittmundhafen → Brandis	1./JG 400			Transferred
		PK+QS	—	14.08.44	Brandis	1./JG 400	Schiebeler	C	Combat sortie
		PK+QS	—	11.10.44	Brandis	1./JG 400	Bott	C	Combat sortie. Aircraft destroyed; Bott injured
BV49	16310058	PK+QT	—	28.09.44	Brandis	1./JG 400	Rösle	C	Combat sortie. Aircraft 60% damaged; Rösle badly injured

Me 163	Werk-nummer	Call sign	Other marking	Date	Place	Unit	Pilot	Flight mode	Remarks
BV50	16310059	PK+QU	—	12.05.44	Wittmundhafen	1./JG 400	Voy (Klemm)	TG	Made two flights same day
		PK+QU	—	13.05.44	Wittmundhafen	1./JG 400	Voy (Klemm)	TR	
		PK+QU	—	15.05.44	Wittmundhafen	1./JG 400	Voy (Klemm)	TG	
		PK+QU	—	18.05.44	Wittmundhafen	1./JG 400	Voy (Klemm)	TG	
		PK+QU	—	19.07.44	Wittmundhafen	1./JG 400	Schiebeler	C	Combat sortie; unsuccessful (Lightning)
BV52	16310061	GH+IU	—	11.05.44	Wittmundhafen	1./JG 400	Voy (Klemm)	TG	
		GH+IU	—	11.06.44	Wittmundhafen	1./JG 400	Zimmermann	C	
		GH+IU	—	18.06.44	Wittmundhafen	1./JG 400	Zimmermann	C	
		GH+IU	—	??.07.44	Wittmundhafen → Brandis	1./JG 400			Transferred
		GH+IU	Y1	??.10.44	Brandis → Stettin-Altdamm	7./JG 400			Transferred. See II./JG 400 for subsequent history
BV54	16310063	GH+IW	—	18.05.44	Wittmundhafen	1./JG 400	Voy (Klemm)	TG	
		GH+IW	—	13.06.44	Wittmundhafen → Rechlin-Lärz	1./JG 400	Zimmermann	TG	Transfer flight
		GH+IW	—	13.06.44	Rechlin-Lärz	1./JG 400	Langer	C	RLM demonstration (Göring, Milch, Italian and Japanese delegations). Participated in formation take-off with BV29 and one unidentified Me 163.
		GH+IW	—	14.06.44	Rechlin-Lärz → Wittmundhafen	1./JG 400	Zimmermann	TG	Transfer flight
		GH+IW	—	17.06.44	Wittmundhafen	1./JG 400	Schiebeler	C	
		GH+IW	—	28.06.44	Wittmundhafen	1./JG 400	Zimmermann	C	
BV55	16310064	GH+IX	—	09.05.44	Wittmundhafen	1./JG 400	Voy (Klemm)	TG	
		GH+IX	—	10.05.44	Wittmundhafen	1./JG 400	Voy (Klemm)	TG	Made three flights same day
		GH+IX	—	15.05.44	Wittmundhafen	1./JG 400	Voy (Klemm)	C	
		GH+IX	—	19.05.44	Wittmundhafen	1./JG 400	Schiebeler	TG	Made two flights same day
		GH+IX	—	19.05.44	Wittmundhafen	1./JG 400	Zimmermann	TG	
		GH+IX	—	07.07.44	Wittmundhafen	1./JG 400	Schiebeler	C	Two combat sorties made same day; both unsuccessful (1st Mustang; 2nd Lightning)
		GH+IX	—	16.07.44	Wittmundhafen	1./JG 400	Schiebeler	C	
		GH+IX	—	20.07.44	Wittmundhafen → Brandis	1./JG 400	Schiebeler	TG	Transferred
BV56	16310065	GH+IY	—	12.05.44	Wittmundhafen	1./JG 400	Voy (Klemm)	TG	
		GH+IY	—	16.05.44	Wittmundhafen	1./JG 400	Voy (Klemm)	TG	
		GH+IY	—	19.05.44	Wittmundhafen	1./JG 400	Voy (Klemm)	C	Made two flight same day
		GH+IY	—	20.05.44	Wittmundhafen	1./JG 400	Voy (Klemm)	C	Made two flights same day
		GH+IY	—	19.06.44	Wittmundhafen	1./JG 400	Zimmermann	C	
BV57	16310066	GH+IZ	—	13.05.44	Wittmundhafen	1./JG 400	Voy (Klemm)	TR	
		GH+IZ	—	28.05.44	Wittmundhafen	1./JG 400	Böhner	C	Aircraft 15% damaged; Böhner injured
BV59	16310068	GN+MB	—	23.05.44	Wittmundhafen	1./JG 400	Voy (Klemm)	TG	
		GN+MB	—	24.05.44	Wittmundhafen	1./JG 400	Voy (Klemm)	TG	Made five flights same day
		GN+MB	—	26.05.44	Wittmundhafen	1./JG 400	Voy (Klemm)	TG + C	Made two flights same day (1st TG; 2nd C)
		GN+MB	—	06.07.44	Wittmundhafen	1./JG 400	Zimmermann	C	Combat sortie

Me 163	Werk-nummer	Call sign	Other marking	Date	Place	Unit	Pilot	Flight mode	Remarks
BV61	16310070	GN+MD	—	07.10.44	Brandis	1./JG 400	Schubert, S.	C	Two combat sorties. Aircraft destroyed on take-off for 2nd sortie; Schubert killed
B	440001	BQ+UD	—	26.05.44	Wittmundhafen	1./JG 400	Voy (Klemm)	TG	
B	440003	BQ+UF	—	02.11.44	Brandis	1./JG 400	Bollenrath	C	Combat sortie. Aircraft destroyed; Bollenrath killed
B	440006	BQ+UI	—	20.02.45	Brandis	?./JG 400		C	Aircraft 30% damaged
B	440007	BQ+UJ	—	02.11.44	Brandis	2./JG 400	Rolly	C	Combat sortie. Aircraft destroyed; Rolly killed
B	440009	BQ+UL	—	26.07.44	Venlo	2./JG 400	Rolly		Aircraft 25% damaged on landing
B	440013	BQ+UP	—	07.10.44	Brandis	2./JG 400	Eisenmann	C	Combat sortie. Aircraft destroyed; Eisenmann killed.
B	440015	BQ+UR	?	09.02.45	Brandis	?./JG 400	Zielsdorf	C	Aircraft 90% damaged; Zielsdorf injured
B	440018	BQ+UU	—	25.05.44	Wittmundhafen	1./JG400	Voy (Klemm)	TG	Made two flights same day
B	440020	BQ+UW	—	26.05.44	Wittmundhafen	1./JG 400	Voy (Klemm)	TG + C	Made two flights same day (1st TG; 2nd C)
B	440165	?	?	07.10.44	Brandis	2./JG 400	Husser	C	Combat sortie. Aircraft 65% damaged; Husser badly injured
B	440172	?	?	19.11.44	Brandis	1./JG 400	Müller	C	Aircraft 50% damaged; Müller injured
B	?	?	W1	24.08.44	Brandis	1./JG 400	Schiebeler	C	Combat sortie; unsuccessful (B-17)
B	440184	DS+VV	W2	11.09.44	Brandis	1./JG 400	Schiebeler	C	Combat sortie; successful (B-17)
		DS+VV	W2	20.09.44	Brandis	1./JG 400	Zimmermann	C	
B		DS+VV	W2	10.02.45	Brandis	1./JG 400	Mohr	C	Aircraft destroyed; Mohr killed
B	?	?	W3	24.08.44	Brandis	1./JG 400	Zimmermann	C	Combat sortie; aborted. Aircraft destroyed on landing
B	?	?	W3	15.09.44	Brandis	1./JG 400	Zimmermann	C	
		?	W3	07.10.44	Brandis	1./JG 400	Schiebeler	C	Combat sortie; successful (B-17)
		?	W3	02.11.44	Brandis	1./JG 400	Schiebeler	C	Combat sortie; unsuccessful (B-17 and P-51)
B	?	?	W4	07.08.44	Brandis	1./JG 400	Schiebeler	C	Combat sortie; unsuccessful (Mosquito)
		?	W4	21.11.44	Brandis	1./JG 400	Zimmermann	C?	
		?	W4	24.11.44	Brandis	1./JG 400	Schiebeler	C	
		?	W4	16.02.45	Brandis	1./JG 400	Schiebeler	C	
		?	W4	??.03.45	Brandis	1./JG 400	Schiebeler	C	Combat sortie
B	?	?	W5	22.11.44	Brandis	1./JG 400	Frömert	C	
B	?	?	W6						No information available

Me 163	Werk-nummer	Call sign	Other marking	Date	Place	Unit	Pilot	Flight mode	Remarks
BV62	16310071	?	W7	28.09.44	Brandis	1./JG 400	Zimmermann	C	Combat sortie
		?	W7	07.10.44	Brandis	1./JG 400	Zimmermann	C	Combat sortie. Landed in Borna
		?	W7	22.11.44	Brandis	1./JG 400	Schiebeler	C	
		?	W7	27.11.44	Brandis	1./JG 400	Krutsch	C	
B	440186	TP+TN	W8	02.11.44	Brandis	1./JG 400	Straznicky	C	Combat sortie. Aircraft destroyed west of Delitzsch; Straznicky killed
BV53	16310062	GH+IV	W9	04.08.44	Brandis	1./JG 400	Schiebeler	C	
B	190598	?	W10	20.02.45	Brandis	1./JG 400	Löscher	C	
		?	W10	22.02.45	Brandis	1./JG 400	Löscher	C	
B	?	?	W11	17.12.44	Brandis	1./JG 400	Schiebeler	TG	
			W11	07.01.45	Brandis	1./JG 400	Schiebeler	TG	
B	?	?	W12	12.10.44	Brandis	1./JG 400	Frömert	C	
B	?	?	W13						No information available
B	?	?	W14	?	Witmundhafen	1./JG 400	?		W14 in Wittmundhafen had different camouflage and markings to that photographed in Brandis
		?	W14	?	Brandis	1./JG 400	?		
B	?	?	W15	05.01.45	Brandis	1./JG 400	Schiebeler	TG	
		?	W15	10.01.45	Brandis	1./JG 400	Schiebeler	TG	
B	?	?	W16	18.02.45	Brandis	1./JG 400	Löscher	C	
		?	W16	19.02.45	Brandis	1./JG 400	Löscher	C	
B	?	?	W17						No information available
B	?	?	W18	08.12.44	Brandis	1./JG 400	Schiebeler	C	
B	?	?	W19-W20						No information available
B	?	?	W21	??.03.45	Brandis	1./JG 400	Schiebeler	C	Combat sortie
		?	W21	19.03.45	Brandis	1./JG 400	Löscher	C	Combat sortie
B-0/R2	191111	SC+VJ	W22	11.02.45	Brandis	1./JG 400	Schüller		Aircraft 15% damaged; Schüller injured
B	440016	BQ+US	B12	28.09.44	Brandis	?./JG 400	Opitz, Reinhard	C	See IV./EJG 2
B	?	?	R6	05.01.45	Brandis	1./JG 400	Krutsch	TG	
B	?	?	R13	24.11.44	Brandis	1./JG 400	Frömert	C	
B	?	?	R26	?	Brandis	1./JG 400	Mentenich	C	Crashed on take-off. Mentenich baled out
B	?	?	G3	16.10.44	Brandis	1./JG 400	Krutsch	C	
B	?	?	G4	22.11.44	Brandis	1./JG 400	Frömert	C	
BV??	163100 ??	?	?	16.08.44	Brandis	1./JG 400	Ryll	C	Combat sortie. Aircraft destroyed near Bad Lausick; Ryll killed
II./JG 400									
BV52	163 100 61	GH+IU	Y1	??.10.44	Brandis → Stettin-Altdamm	7./JG 400		C	Transferred. See I./JG 400
			Y1	??.02.45	Stettin-Altdamm → Salzwedel	7./JG 400			Transferred
			Y1	??.02.45	Salzwedel → Nordholz	7./JG 400			Transferred

Me 163	Werk-nummer	Call sign	Other marking	Date	Place	Unit	Pilot	Flight mode	Remarks
			Y1	10.04.45	Nordholz	7./JG 400	Opitz, Reinhard		
			Y1	12.04.45	Nordholz → Husum	7./JG 400	Opitz, Reinhard	C	Transfer flight
			Y1	19.04.45	Husum	7./JG 400	Opitz, Reinhard	C	Last entry in Opitz's log book
			Y1	08.05.45	Husum	7./JG 400	—	—	Brought to UK and handed over to the French *Armée de l'Air* in March 1946
B	?	?	Y2–Y5						No information available
B	191316	?	Y6	08.05.45	Husum	?./JG 400	—	—	
B	?	?	Y7	13.03.45	Nordholz	7./JG 400	Opitz, Reinhard	C	
		?	Y7	06.04.45	Nordholz	7./JG 400	Frömert	C	
		?	Y7	??.04.45	Nordholz → Husum	7./JG 400	—	—	Transferred
		?	Y7	27.04.45	Husum	7./JG 400	Frömert	C	
B	?	?	Y8	29.11.44	Stargard	7./JG 400	Opitz, Reinhard	TG	
B	?	?	Y9						No information available
B	?	?	Y10	05.04.45	Nordholz	7./JG 400	Opitz, Reinhard	C	
		?	Y10	06.04.45	Nordholz	7./JG 400	?	?	Towed aloft by Hptm Frömert in Bf 110, D5+VZ
		?	Y10	10.04.45	Nordholz	7./JG400	Frömert	C	
B	191454	?	Y11	08.05.45	Husum	?./JG 400	—	—	
B	?	?	Y12						No information available
B	?	?	Y13	08.05.45	Husum	?./JG 400	—	—	Captured by RAF Regiment
		?	Y13	?	Husum → Farnborough	AM	—	—	Delivered to RAE Farnborough
		?	AM203	10.03.46	Farnborough Dieppe	AM	—	—	Delivered to AA, France
B	?	?	Y14						No information available
B-1a	191659	?	Y15	08.05.45	Husum	?./JG 400	—	—	
B	?	?	Y16–Y24						No information available
B	191914	?	?	08.05.45	Husum	6./JG 400	—	—	
B-1a	191917	?	Y25	08.05.45	Husum	?./JG 400	—	—	
B	?	?	Y26	08.05.45	Husum	6./JG 400	—	—	
B	?	?	B2	13.01.45	Stargard	7./JG 400	Opitz, Reinhard	C	
		?	B2	15.01.45	Stettin	7./JG 400	Opitz, Reinhard	C	
		?	B2	19.02.45	Salzwedel	7./JG 400	Opitz, Reinhard	C	
B	?	?	R8	25.12.44	Stargard	?./JG 400	?	?	Towed aloft by Hptm Frömert in Bf 110, White 8

Erg.St./JG 400

AV10	1630000007	CD+IO	—	03.08.44	Brandis	ErgSt/JG 400	Frömert	C	
		CD+IO	—	09.08.44	Brandis	ErgSt/JG 400	Krutsch	C	
AV11	1630000008	CD+IP	—	08.08.44	Brandis	ErgSt/JG 400	Krutsch	C	
AV13	1630000010	CD+IR	—	03.08.44	Brandis	ErgSt/JG 400	Krutsch	TG	
BV1	16310010	KE+SX	—	25.07.44	Brandis	ErgSt/JG 400	Krutsch	TG	
		KE+SX	—	28.07.44	Brandis	ErgSt/JG 400	Krutsch	TG	
		KE+SX	—	31.07.44	Brandis	ErgSt/JG 400	Krutsch	TG	
		KE+SX	—	05.08.44	Brandis	ErgSt/JG 400	Krutsch	TG	

Me 163	Werk-nummer	Call sign	Other marking	Date	Place	Unit	Pilot	Flight mode	Remarks
		KE+SX	—	10.08.44	Brandis	ErgSt/JG 400	Krutsch	TG	Made two flights same day
		KE+SX	—	14.08.44	Brandis	ErgSt/JG 400	Krutsch	TG	
		KE+SX	—	??.04.45	Esperstedt?				Captured by US Army. Transported to USA at end of the war
BV4	16310013	VD+EN	—	31.07.44	Brandis	ErgSt/JG 400	Krutsch	TG	
		VD+EN	—	12.08.44	Brandis	ErgSt/JG 400	Krutsch	TG	
		VD+EN	—	14.08.44	Brandis	ErgSt/JG 400	Opitz, Reinhard	TG	
		VD+EN	—	15.08.44	Brandis	ErgSt/JG 400	Opitz, Reinhard	TG	Made two flights same day
		VD+EN	—	17.08.44	Brandis	ErgSt/JG 400	Opitz, Reinhard	TG	
		VD+EN	—	10.09.44	Brandis	ErgSt/JG 400	Hauss	TG	
		VD+EN	—	11.09.44	Brandis	ErgSt/JG 400	Hauss	TG	
		VD+EN	—	03.10.44	Brandis	ErgSt/JG 400	Pancherz (Ju)	TG	Made three flights same day
		VD+EN	—	04.10.44	Brandis	ErgSt/JG 400	Pancherz (Ju)	TG	
		VD+EN	—	07.10.44	Brandis	ErgSt/JG 400	Pancherz (Ju)	TG	Made two flights same day
		VD+EN	—	11.10.44	Brandis	ErgSt/JG 400	Kuhn	TG	
BV8	16310017	VD+ER	—	14.08.44	Brandis	ErgSt/JG 400	Opitz, Reinhard	TG	
		VD+ER	—	17.08.44	Brandis	ErgSt/JG 400	Opitz, Reinhard	TG	
		VD+ER	—	09.09.44	Brandis	ErgSt/JG 400	Hauss	TG	
		VD+ER	—	10.09.44	Brandis	ErgSt/JG 400	Hauss	TG	
		VD+ER	—	11.09.44	Brandis	ErgSt/JG 400	Hauss	TG	
		VD+ER	—	12.09.44	Brandis	ErgSt/JG 400	Hauss	TG	
		VD+ER	—	12.10.44	Brandis	ErgSt/JG 400	Kuhn	TG	Made two flights same day

IV./EJG 2

Me 163	Werk-nummer	Call sign	Other marking	Date	Place	Unit	Pilot	Flight mode	Remarks
B	?	?	2	12.11.44	Udetfeld	14./EJG 2	Löscher	TG	
		?	2	05.12.44	Udetfeld	14./EJG 2	Hauss	TG	
B	?	?	3	05.11.44	Udetfeld	14./EJG 2	Hauss	TG	
B	?	?	6	05.12.44	Udetfeld	14./EJG 2	Hauss	TG	
B	?	?	7	06.11.44	Udetfeld	14./EJG 2	Löscher	TG	
		?	7	12.11.44	Udetfeld	14./EJG 2	Löscher	TG	
		?	7	13.11.44	Udetfeld	14./EJG 2	Löscher	TG	
		?	7	14.11.44	Udetfeld	14./EJG 2	Hauss	TG	
		?	7	25.11.44	Udetfeld	14./EJG 2	Hauss	TG	
		?	7	07.12.44	Udetfeld	14./EJG 2	Hauss	TG	
		?	7	08.12.44	Udetfeld	14./EJG 2	Hauss	TG	
B	?	?	9	05.11.44	Udetfeld	14./EJG 2	Hauss	TG	
		?	9	17.01.45	Sprottau	14./EJG 2	Löscher	TG	
B	440016	BQ+US	B12	17.12.44	Udetfeld	13./EJG 2	Giesl	C	Aircraft destroyed east of Tschenstochau (Poland); Giesl killed. See I./JG 400
B	191110	SC+VI	?	10.12.44	Sprottau	14./EJG 2	Löscher	TG	
		SC+VI	?	23.12.44	Sprottau	14./EJG 2	Löscher	TG	
		SC+VI	?	23.12.44	Sprottau	14./EJG 2	Jung	TG	
		SC+VI	?	28.12.44	Sprottau	14./EJG 2	Löscher	TG	
B	191121	SC+VT	?	13.12.44	Sprottau	14./EJG 2	Löscher	TG	
		SC+VT	?	17.12.44	Sprottau	14./EJG 2	Jung	TG	
B	191320	?	?	17.12.44	Sprottau	14./EJG 2	Löscher	TG	
		?	?	23.12.44	Sprottau	14./EJG 2	Jung	TG	

Me 163	Werk-nummer	Call sign	Other marking	Date	Place	Unit	Pilot	Flight mode	Remarks
B	?	?	W42	??.04.45	Esperstedt?	??./EJG 2			Captured by US Army Transported to USA at end of the war.
B	?	?	W51	14.01.45	Sprottau	14./EJG 2	Jung	TG	
		?	W51	15.01.45	Sprottau	14./EJG 2	Jung	TG	Made two flights same day
B	?	?	W52						No information available
B	?	?	W53	15.01.45	Sprottau	14./EJG 2	Löscher	TG	
		?	W53	17.01.45	Sprottau	14./EJG 2	Löscher	TG	
B	?	?	W54	??.04.45	Esperstedt?				Captured by US Army. Transported to USA at end of the war. At least fin used in reassembly of Me 163 numbered FE495
B	?	?	W55	15.01.45	Sprottau	14./EJG 2	Löscher	TG	
		?	W55	20.01.45	Sprottau	14./EJG 2	Löscher	TG	
B	?	?	W56						No information available
B	?	?	W57	20.01.45	Sprottau	14./EJG 2	Löscher	TG	
B	?	?	W58	20.01.45	Sprottau	14./EJG 2	Löscher	C	
B	?	?	W59	04.01.45	Udetfeld	14./EJG 2	Hauss	TG	
B	191301	?	—	??.04.45	Esperstedt?				Flight tested by Karl Voy (Klemm), *Baugesellschaft Antonienhof*, Oranienburg, 3 December 1944. Captured by US Army. Transported to USA at end of the war and flown May 1946. Numbered T-2-500/FE500
B	191302	?	?	12.12.44	Sprottau	14./EJG 2	Löscher	TG	
		?	?	22.12.44	Sprottau	14./EJG 2	Jung	TG	
B	191320	?	?	17.12.44	Sprottau	14./EJG 2	Löscher	TG	
		?	?	23.12.44	Sprottau	14./EJG 2	Jung	TG	

APPENDIX 5

Me 163 ARMAMENT

MG 151/20

The Me 163B was initially armed with two MG 151/20
machine guns mounted in the wing roots. Ground firing and
the first in-flight firing tests were conducted by
Messerschmitt at Lechfeld with Me 163B V2 Wk-Nr.
16310011 VD+EL in October and November 1942 before the
aircraft was handed over to *Erprobungskommando* (EKdo) 16
for further trials. The MG 151/20 was fitted as standard
armament on Me 163Bs up to and including BV44, except
BV6, BV10 and BV16. Official documents state that all
Me 163Bs delivered after and including BV46 were to be
completed with the MK 108 installation; BV45 was an

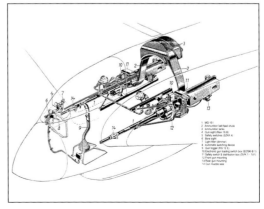

MG 151/20 installation

exception to this order and was fitted with the MK 108. Firing trials with two additional MG 151/20 mounted in pods under the wings were conducted by EKdo 16 at Bad Zwischenahn in December 1942. The installation proved operationally unacceptable and the idea for this form of additional armament was abandoned.

MG 151/20: calibre, 20 mm; rate of fire, 720 rounds/minute; muzzle velocity, 695-785m/s (dependent on type of ammunition). Manufacturer: Waffenfabrik Mauser AG. Quantity of ammunition carried by the Me 163: 80 rounds per gun.

MK 108

The initial in-flight firing trials with the MK 108 cannon fitted to an Me 163B were conducted by EKdo 16 at Bad Zwischenahn and by 1./JG 400 at Wittmundhafen with BV16, Wk-Nr. 16310025, in April 1944. (Me 163B V16 was destroyed in an emergency landing on 21 April 1944; the aircraft's pilot, Hauptmann Robert Olejnik *Staffelkapitän* 1./JG 400 was badly injured.) All aircraft delivered after and including BV45 were fitted with the MK 108. The MG 151 and MK 108 installations were not interchangeable.

MK 108: calibre, 30 mm; rate of fire, 600 rounds/minute; muzzle velocity, 525m/s. Manufacturer: Rheinmetall-Borsig. Quantity of ammunition carried by the Me 163: 60 rounds per cannon.

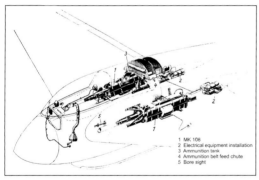

1 MK 108
2 Electrical equipment installation
3 Ammunition tank
4 Ammunition belt feed chute
5 Bore sight

MK 108 installation

SG 500 *Jägerfaust*

SG 500 *Jägerfaust* was a recoilless weapon which fired shells vertically upwards from a rifled barrel, the barrel being ejected downwards to counterbalance the explosive force propelling the shell. The barrel was restrained during flight with shear pins which were severed when the weapon was fired. The weapon was triggered by the shadow cast by the target on a photo-electric cell as the Me 163 flew 150-100 metres beneath it. It was proposed to install five barrels in the wing in line astern but testing with suitably modified Me 163s was conducted with only four or five barrels per wing.

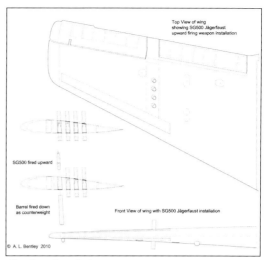

Top View of wing showing SG500 Jägerfaust upward firing weapon installation

SG500 fired upward

Barrel fired down as counterweight

Front View of wing with SG500 Jägerfaust installation

© A. L. Bentley 2010

Jägerfaust **installation**

According to Wolfgang Späte, the *Jägerfaust* was invented and patented by Oberleutnant Gustav Korff – *Aktenzeichen 68b 22 Nr. 11019/44 Geheim (FVD)* – and Hugo Schneider AG (HASAG) delivered 32 sets of these weapons to Brandis in the autumn of 1944.

The first two test flights were made with BV45 equipped with the *Jägerfaust* supplied by HASAG in November 1944. These flights showed that the weapon installation did not in any way affect the aircraft's performance, take-off or manoeuvring capability. In both cases, the weapon was manually triggered by the pilot, Leutnant August Hachtel. These tests were conducted with 2 cm-calibre shells.

The installation of the photo-electric 'eye' proved more difficult and, in order to be able to at least check that it worked properly, the 'eye' was installed in front of the Moran radio aerial near the aircraft's ammunition bay.

Due to of a shortage of fuel for the Me 163s, tests were continued in December to check the function of the 'eye' with a Fw 190, in which the latter flew above a stationary armed Me 163 and *Jägerfaust* barrels positioned 20 metres alongside it.

In order to prove that the weapon would fire in flight, two poles about 25 metres long were positioned close to the end of the runway at Brandis and a sheet 40 metres long and one metre wide was stretched between the poles. The pilot was required to fly between the poles and under the sheet. A preliminary test was made with the Fw 190 and the pilot experienced no difficulty in performing this manoeuvre. The test was repeated with live ammunition triggered by the pilot himself and all six 5cm barrels fired, the barrels hitting the hard ground and bouncing back behind and to almost the same height as the aircraft. No further tests with the Fw 190 were made because of the danger to the pilot and the aircraft in continuing them.

August Hachtel joined the Luftwaffe in November 1935. On completion of pilot training (July 1937-August 1939) he was posted to 7./StG 51 (later renamed 4./StG 1), remaining with that squadron until November 1942. He was awarded the *Deutsches Kreuz* on 17 October 1941 and the *Ritterkreuz* on 6 January 1942 (credited with the destruction of 32 tanks, and ships totalling 32,000 registered tons). During the autumn of 1942, he flew 500 sorties over Russia. From November 1942 to January 1943, he served with *Ergänzungsstaffel*/ StG 1 and from January 1943 to April 1944 with 2./SG 103 as a flying instructor. He was promoted to Leutnant in August 1943 and joined EKdo 16 at Bad Zwischenahn in April 1944. Hachtel transferred with that unit to Brandis in October 1944, where he conducted trials with the *Jägerfaust* in December (*JG 400 Archive*)

This wrecked Me 163, found at Brandis, was one of at least three aircraft fitted with the SG 500 *Jägerfaust*. The three holes in the port wing, where the *Jägerfaust* was installed, are masked by the German wing cross. Three *Jägerfaust* barrels were also fitted in the starboard wing (*JG 400 Archive*)

Leutnant Hachtel conducted the same test with Me 163B V45 on 24 December. Hachtel took off with the aircraft partly fuelled, climbed to a height of about 3,000 metres, levelled off and flew from west to east towards the 'goal'. He took off in an easterly direction towards the sun and then turned away with the sun behind him before diving to make his approach to the target. During the turn, the aircraft's wing must have cast a deep shadow over the optical cell because the weapon prematurely detonated at a height of about 300 metres. The shock from the muzzles of the barrels shattered the aircraft's canopy and the pilot received a hard knock on his head. He managed to land while still dazed and with the sun in his eyes. The damage to the aircraft was assessed at 40%; the pilot suffered severe back injuries and concussion. (BV45 was afterwards repaired but not used again for *Jägerfaust* trials.)

Afterwards, tests with the 5cm barrels were continued with them fitted to the Fw 190. During the initial tests, the muzzle shock either shattered or damaged the aircraft's canopy. This problem was resolved by moving the weapons further outboard and adding a mechanism that allowed the barrels to be fired one after another.

Experience with the vertically firing weapon gained during December revealed that, on very cold days, the muzzle shock would shatter the canopies of both the Fw 190 and the Me 163. It was discovered that the problem lay in the method of firing the weapon and HASAG, therefore, introduced a timer which allowed the shells to be fired not as a single salvo but very quickly one after another at intervals of 3/1,000th of a second. In addition, the distance between the weapon installation and the canopy was slightly increased. No further problems occurred during flight trials conducted in January 1945 after these modifications had been made to the Fw 190.

On completion of the trials with the Fw 190, eight 5-cm barrels were installed in an Me 163. The first flight and firing trials with this installation took place early in February 1945.

Another of the wrecked Me 163s at Brandis, in this case revealing the location of four *Jägerfaust* barrels (*JG 400 Archive*)

COLOUR PLATES COMMENTARY

The authors have selected the colour profiles to illustrate the relatively large number of variations in camouflage schemes and styles of call signs applied to the following aircraft.

1

DFS 194, Peenemünde, November 1939
This tailless aircraft can be considered as the immediate precursor of the Me 163A. As originally designed at the *Deutsche Forschungsanstalt für Segelflug*, Darmstadt, in 1936 it was fitted with a wing planform similar to the DFS 39 and a pusher propeller, in which form it was extensively tested in the wind tunnels at the *Aerodynamische Versuchsanstalt* in Göttingen from June 1937 to July 1938. In the autumn of 1937 the DFS was requested to examine the possibility of fitting a rocket engine being developed by Hellmuth Walter KG at Kiel to the DFS 194. The subsequently modified design produced by Alexander Lippisch, Josef Hubert and Fritz Krämer while still at the DFS was taken by Lippisch to Messerschmitt in Augsburg when he joined that company on 2 January 1939. The DFS 194 was completed at Augsburg and transferred to Peenemünde, where it made its first gliding flight on 28 July 1939 piloted by Heini Dittmar. Powered flights were made between 16 October 1939 and 30 November 1940, also by Dittmar.

2

Me 163 AV4 Wk-Nr. 1630000001 'KE+SW' of the *Erprobungsstelle*, Peenemünde October 1941
The first of ten prototypes built by Messerschmitt AG in Augsburg. Its first towed flight took place at Augsburg on 13 February 1941; it was subsequently delivered to the *Erprobungsstelle* at Peenemünde where it made its first powered flight on 13 August 1941. All test flights were made by Heini Dittmar. On 2 October 1941 Dittmar established an unofficial world speed record with AV4 of 1,003 km/h for which he was promoted to the rank of Flugkapitän and awarded the Lilienthal Prize for Aviation Research. Ten months later, in August 1942, AV4 was handed over to the *Erprobungskommando* 16 at Peenemünde and then transferred one year later with that unit to Bad Zwischenahn, where it was used for training. Pilots' log books reveal that it was flown only as a glider while at Bad Zwischenahn. The last known flight with AV4 was made in April 1944.

3

Me 163 AV10 Wk-Nr. 1630000010 'CD+IO' of *Erprobungskommando* 16, Peenemünde, spring 1943
Used by *Erprobungskommando* 16 at Peenemünde for trials with the undercarriage dolly. These were conducted by Oberleutnant Rudi Opitz. The aircraft was transferred to Bad Zwischenahn in August 1943 and there used for training pilots ('sharp' take-offs and gliding landings). In July 1944, it was transferred to Brandis, where it was to become one of six aircraft allocated to *Ergänzungsstaffel*/JG 400. This unit was moved to Udetfeld in November 1944 under the command of Oberleutnant Adolf Niemeyer and, a little later, renamed 13./EJG 2. In December 1944, AV10 was used for flight trials with 24 wing-mounted, dummy R4M (*Rakete 4kg Minengefechtskopf*) rockets. The aircraft's fate is not known.

4

Me 163 BV35 Wk-Nr. 16310044 'GH+IN' of *Erprobungskommando* 16, Bad Zwischenahn, October 1944
This aircraft was used by *Erprobungskommando* 16 primarily for FuG 25a radio trials. It was among EKdo 16's aircraft transferred from Bad Zwischenahn to Brandis in October 1944. While still at Bad Zwischenahn it was repainted and given the call sign C1+13. An unconfirmed report states that it was flown in combat by Unteroffizier Tegtmeier, (EKdo 16) on 2 November 1944. On the following day it was again flown by Tegtmeier to test automatic target homing equipment and on 5 November the aircraft was badly damaged by Feldwebel Hans-Günther Heinzel (EKdo 16) in a misjudged landing at Brandis.

5

Me 163 BV45 Wk-Nr. 16310054 'PK+QP' of *Erprobungskommando* 16, Bad Zwischenahn, May 1944
This aircraft served with EKdo 16; the earliest record of its presence at Bad Zwischenahn, to where it had been delivered, was on 30 May 1944 when it was recorded that it was 15% damaged in the Eighth Air Force bombing raid.

6

Me 163 BV45 Wk-Nr. 16310054 'C1+05' of *Erprobungskommando* 16, Bad Zwischenahn, July 1944
The aircraft was completely repainted and allotted the call sign C1+05 in July 1944 (c.f. plate 5). In this guise it appears to have been flown mainly by Leutnant August Hachtel, RK, DK. The aircraft was transferred to Brandis in October 1944. The aircraft flown by Hachtel was used in development trials of the *Jägerfaust* in late 1944.

7

Me 163B Wk-Nr. 440014 of 2./JG 400, Venlo, August 1944
This aircraft was built by Hanns Klemm Flugzeugbau in Böblingen and test flown by Karl Voy at Jesau on 27 July 1944 before delivery to 2./JG 400 at Venlo. It was allocated the call sign BQ+UQ, but was probably not painted with this marking (some aircraft delivered by Klemm to Jesau were painted blue/grey and marked with call signs; others were painted with mottled camouflage without call signs)

8

Me 163B-0 Wk-Nr. 190598 'White 10' of 1./JG 400, Brandis, February 1945
According to the *Werknummer* this aircraft was from the first batch of 29 Me 163Bs built by Junkers and completed by the Junkers subsidiary, Baugesellschaft Antonienhof, located at Oranienburg. Leutnant Hans-Ludwig Löscher's flight log book records that he flew this aircraft while serving with 1./JG 400 at Brandis in February 1945.

9

Me 163B 'White 14' of 1./JG 400, Brandis, February 1945
The camouflage markings indicate that this aircraft was built by Klemm. The aircraft's *Werknummer* was painted in small characters at the base of the fin just forward of the rudder but its actual identity cannot be discerned from the available photographs of this aircraft. 'White 14' was one of few painted with 1./JG 400's 'Flying Flea' emblem, which adorned only the port side of these aircraft.

10

Me 163B 'White 14' of 1./JG 400, Brandis, March 1945

During its service with JG 400, the aircraft was repainted with a different mottled camouflage pattern, during the course of which the 'Flying Flea' emblem was obliterated and the squadron number '14' was applied with thinner strokes. It was portrayed in a training film made at Brandis.

11

Me 163 BV52 Wk-Nr. 163100061 'GH+IU' 'Yellow 1' of 7./JG 400, Stettin-Altdamm, October 1944

This aircraft was built by Messerschmitt and completed by Klemm at Jesau. It was delivered to Wittmundhafen and there flight tested by Karl Voy on 11 May 1944 before being handed over to 1./JG 400. It is recorded that it was flown by Feldwebel Rudolf Zimmermann, 1./JG 400, in June. Zimmermann transferred with 1./JG 400 to Brandis. The aircraft was afterwards handed over to 7./JG 400 when that squadron was formed in Stettin-Altdamm in October 1944. 'Yellow 1' was flown by Leutnant Reinhard Opitz, *Staffelkapitän* 7./JG 400, at Nordholz and Husum in April 1945, and not flown in combat.

12

Me 163B 'Yellow 2' of 7./JG 400?, Husum, May 1945

Previous identity and service record unknown. Photographed at Husum.

13

Me 163B 'Yellow 7' of 7./JG 400, Husum, May 1945

Flown by Leutnant Reinhard Opitz, *Staffelkapitän* 7./JG 400, and Oberleutnant Herbert Frömert, 7./JG 400, in March and April 1945. Not flown in combat.

14

Me 163B 'White 42' of IV./EJG 2?, Esperstedt, May 1945

Previous identity and service record unknown. Found by US Army at Esperstedt along with other Me 163s from IV./EJG 2 and transported by lorry to the Captured Aircraft Park at Merseburg, from where it was transported via Kassel-Rothwesten to Freeman Army Air Field, Seymour, Indiana, USA. The squadron emblem, 'Shooting Star,' was painted on both sides of the nose (mirror images). This aircraft was fitted with MG 151 machine guns, and had a faired vent on the tail cone and mottled camouflage pattern, indicating that it might have been one of the early prototypes delivered by Klemm.

15

Me 163S of the Flight Research Institute, Moscow, autumn 1945

Previous identity and service record unknown. This aircraft was possibly captured by the Soviet Army at Berlin-Staaken, where Deutsche Lufthansa AG added a second cockpit to standard production Me 163Bs for conversion training purposes. It is reported that the USSR captured seven two-seaters, one of which was tested in a large wind tunnel at TsAGI and another test flown as a glider (No 94) at the Flight Research Institute, near Moscow. It is recorded that the Me 163S was flown by Karl Voy, at Oranienburg or Rangsdorf, flight tested by Leutnant Bott/Hauptmann Falderbaum, 1./JG 400, and Obergefreiter Gerhard Stolle/Obergefreiter Franz Kalt, 2./JG 400, at Brandis, and Bernhard Hohmann/Theodor Erb at the *Erprobungsstelle* Peenemünde. The Me 163S at Brandis was not among the wrecked aircraft found by the US Army when it captured the airfield on 16 April 1945.

BIBLIOGRAPHY

ALEXANDER LIPPISCH
LIPPISCH, A.M., *Erinnerungen* (Luftfahrtverlag Axel Zuerl, Steinebach-Wörthsee, 1978).

LIPPISCH, A. AND TRENKLE, F., *Ein Dreieck fliegt. Die Entwicklung der Delta-Flugzeuge bis 1945* (Motorbuch Verlag, Stuttgart, 1976). [Translation: *The Delta Wing. History and Development* (Iowa State University Press, Ames, Iowa, 1981)]

LIPPISCH, A., '*Über der Entwicklung der schwanzlosen Flugzeuge* [The development of tailless aircraft],' DAL Report 1064/43 gKdos, *Schriften der deutschen Akademie der Luftfahrtforschung* (DAL), Berlin, 1943.

WOODS, R.J. (ED), 'Survey of Messerschmitt Factory and Functions, Oberammergau, Germany,' Air Technical Intelligence Report F-IR-6-RE, Air Materiel Command, Wright Field, Dayton, Ohio, 1 August 1946.

Me 163
SPÄTE, W. AND BATESON, R.P., *Messerschmitt Me 163 Komet* (Profile 225, Profile Publications Ltd, Windsor, Berkshire, 1971).

ETHELL, J.L., *Komet. The Messerschmitt 163* (Ian Allan Ltd, London, 1978). [Translation: *Messerschmitt Komet. Entwicklung und Einsatz des ersten Raketenjägers* (Motorbuch Verlag, Stuttgart, 1980)]

ETHELL, J.L. AND PRICE, A. *The German Jets in Combat* (Jane's Publishing Company, London, UK, 1979).

SPÄTE, W., *Der streng geheime Vogel. Erprobung an der Schallgrenze* (Verlag für Wehrwissenschaften, Munich, 1983). [Translation: *Top Secret Bird. The Luftwaffe's Me-163 Comet* (Pictorial Histories Publishing Co, Missoula, Montana, 1989)]

BUTLER, P.H., *War Prizes: An illustrated survey of German, Italian and Japanese aircraft brought to Allied countries during and after the Second World War* (Midland Counties Publications, UK, 1998)

RANSOM, S. AND CAMMANN, H.-H., *Me 163 Rocket Interceptor* (Classic Publications, Crowborough, UK, Vol.1, 2002, Vol.2, 2003).

(-), '*Me 163-B. Kurze technische Beschreibung, Leistungen,*' Memorandum 4042/44 g.Kdos., from the office of the General der Jagdflieger, Berlin-Kladow, 19 August 1944.

JAGDGESCHWADER JG 400, ERGANZUNGSSTAFFEL/JG 400 AND IV./EJG 2

(-), 'Stand der Aufstellung der Verbände Me 163,' Memorandum 4045/44 g.Kdos. from the office of the General der Jagdflieger, Kladow-Hottengrund, 19 August 1944.

VON CRIEGERN, - , 'Aufstellung 4./J.G. 400,' File No. Az.11b16.10, Memorandum No. 12871/44 g.Kdos., Headquarters OKL, Generalquartiermeister, 4 September 1944.

GALLAND, A., Memorandum concerning operational readiness of Me 163, No. 4041/14 g.Kdos., Berlin-Kladow, 8 September 1944.

GALLAND, A., 'Vollmacht,' Memorandum 5045/44 g.Kdos., OKL General der Jagdflieger, Berlin-Kladow, 14 October 1944.

VON CRIEGERN, - , 'Umbennung 3. und 4./J.G. 400; Aufstellung Stab II./J.G. 400, 3. and 7./J.G. 400,' File No. Az.11b16.10, Memorandum No. 14332/44 g.Kdos., Headquarters OKL, Generalquartiermeister, 12 November 1944.

VON CRIEGERN, - , 'Aufstellung von Geschwaderstäben bzw. Jagdstaffeln,' File No. Az.11b16.10, Memorandum No. 15075/44 g.Kdos., Headquarters OKL, Generalquartiermeister, 27 December 1944.

Generalquartiermeister Lw, 6. Abteilung, 'Bestandsmeldungen Jagdverbände (Erg.) für November und Dezember 1944,' no place, no date.

Generalquartiermeister Lw, 6. Abteilung, 'Lagekarten „Aufmarsch der Luftverteidigungsverbände der Luftwaffe' für den Zeitraum 26.07.1944-27.02.1945.'

VON CRIEGERN, - , 'Auflösung Stab J.G. 400,' File No. Az.11b16.10, Memorandum No. 1017/45 g.Kdos., Headquarters OKL, Generalquartiermeister, 7 March 1945

(-), 'Einsatzbereitschaft der flg. Verbände im Bereich Lfl.Kdo.Reich. Stand: 11.4.1945, abends,' Report, Chefgruppe Generalquartiermeister, Headquarters, 12 April 1945.

DITTMANN, F., Der Einsatzflughafen Esperstedt der deutschen Luftwaffe 1935 bis 1945, in Kelbraer Heimatgeschichtshefte, Heft Nr. 5 (Graphischer Kunstverlag 'Kyffhäuser,' Kelbra, 1995).

Me 163 OPERATIONS

WALTER, E., ''Kill' successes with the Me 163,' MoS TIL Translation TP 218a, no date.

ANON, 'Enemy Jet Propelled Aircraft,' Report D-Z-63, Headquarters 2nd Bombardment Division, 25 August 1944.

ANON, 'German jet propelled aircraft. Analysis of their tactics, types, and bases of operation,' Report, Headquarters 65th Fighter Wing, 24 November 1944.

DREW, R.B., 'Third Allied Intelligence Report on German Jet Operations,' Allied Intelligence Report, ca. February 1945.

UNITED STATES ARMY AIR FORCE OPERATIONS

USAAF 8th Air Force Intops Summaries: 28 Jul 44 (No.89), 29 Jul 44 (90), 16 Aug 44 (108), 24 Aug 44 (116), 11 Sep 44 (134), 12 Sep 44 (135), 13 Sep 44 (136), 28 Sep 44 (151), 5 Oct 44 (158), 7 Oct 44 (160), 2 Nov 44 (186), 25 Nov 44 (209), 30 Nov 44 (214), 12 Dec 44 (226), 6 Feb 45 (282), 9 Feb 45 (285), 15 Feb 45 (291), 2 Mar 45 (306), 3 Mar 45 (307), 26 Mar 45 (330), 31 Mar 45 (335).

AIRFIELDS

ANON, 'Development of Airfields for Me 163s and Me 262s,' AI2(b) Report, 14 October 1944.

REINICKE, J., Chronik des Flugplatzes Zwischenahn (Cramer-Druck, Buchdruckerei Eberhard Ries, Westerstede, 1986).

RIES, K. AND WOLFGANG DIERICH, W., Fliegerhorste und Einsatzhäfen der Luftwaffe - Planskizzen 1935 - 1945 (Motorbuch-Verlag, Stuttgart, 1993).

STÜWE, B., Peenemünde-West (Bechtle Verlag, Esslingen, 1995).

RANSOM, S., Zwischen Leipzig und der Mulde. Flugplatz Brandis 1935-1945 (Stedinger Verlag, Lemwerder, Germany, 1996).

WEAPON INSTALLATIONS

Me 163B handbooks

THALER, A., Sonderauftrag Senkrechtwaffen, Memorandum, 637/44 g.Kdos., from EKdo 16 Waldpolenz to KdE Rechlin 30 November 1944.

GROSHOLZ, - , Ref. Jägerfaust trials, Memorandum, 2313/44 g.Kdos., from KdE Rechlin to OKL Genst.Gen.Qu.6.Abt.IA Berlin, 6 December 1944.

GROSHOLZ, - , Ref. 'Monatsbericht Nov.,' Memorandum, 2734/44 g.Kdos., from KdE Rechlin to EKdo 16, 8 December 1944.

DAHL, - , 'Wochenbericht von 4.12.-10.12.44,' Telex, 1823/44 geh., from EKdo 16 Waldpolenz to KdE Rechlin, 11 December 1944.

SCHLIEPHAKE, H., Flugzeugbewaffnung. Die Bordwaffen der Luftwaffe von den Anfängen bis zur Gegenwart (Motorbuch Verlag, Stuttgart, 1977).

RdL AND ObdL, MK 108 3cm-Flugzeugmaschinenkanone 108, Waffenhandbuch (Stand Oktober 1943), Document No D.(Luft) T.6108, Technisches Amt GL/C, Berlin, 25 October 1943.

Appendix 2, EKdo 16 Monthly Report, Brandis, 5 January 1945.

RCAF Operational Records, 6th Group, 10 April 1945.

The RCAF Overseas. The Sixth Year, pp.162-163.

Operational Record Book, 309 (Polish) Squadron RAF, 10 April 1945.

ABBREVIATIONS

AVA	*Aerodynamische Versuchsanstalt* Göttingen eV (Aerodynamic Test Establishment, Göttingen)		**KGrzbV**	*Kampfgruppe zur besonderen Verwendung* (Special duties battle group)
BMW	Bayerische Motorenwerke		**LLG**	*Luftlandegeschwader* (Glider assault wing)
C	Conventional 'sharp' take-off (Appendix 4)		**NSDAP**	*Nationalsozialistische Deutsche Arbeiter Partei* (German National Socialist Workers [Nazi] Party)
DFC	Distinguished Flying Cross		**NSFK**	*Nationalsozialistisches Fliegerkorps* (National Socialist Flying Corps)
DFS	*Deutsches Forschungsinstitut für Segelflug.* In 1937 renamed *Deutsche Forschungsanstalt für Segelflug Ernst Udet eV* (German Research Institute / Establishment of Gliding Flight, Darmstadt)		**ObdL**	Oberbefehlshaber der Luftwaffe (Commander-in-Chief, German Air Force)
DK	*Deutsches Kreuz* (German Cross)		**OKL**	*Oberkommando der Luftwaffe* (Headquarters, German Air Force)
DLV	*Deutscher Luftsport-Verband* (German Aero Club Association)		**PRU**	Photographic Reconnaissance Unit
DSO	Distinguished Service Order		**RAF**	Royal Air Force
EJG	*Ergänzungsjagdgeschwader* (Auxiliary fighter wing)		**RCAF**	Royal Canadian Air Force
EK	*Eisernes Kreuz* (Iron Cross)		**RdL**	Reichsminister der Luftfahrt (German Minister of Aviation)
EKdo	*Erprobungskommando* (Operational trials unit)		**RK**	*Ritterkreuz* (Knight's Cross)
FuG	*Funkgerät* (Radio equipment)		**RLM**	*Reichsluftfahrtministerium* (German Air Ministry)
HASAG	Hugo Schneider AG (German phonetic abbreviation)		**RRG**	*Rhön-Rossitten-Gesellschaft eV* (Rhön-Rossitten Society, Wasserkuppe)
HWA	*Heereswaffenamt* (Army Ordnance Office, Berlin)		**SG**	*Sondergerät* (Special equipment)
HWK	Hellmuth Walter Kiel		**StG**	*Sturzkampfgeschwader/Stukageschwader* (Dive-bomber wing)
ISTUS	*Internationale Studienkommission für Segelflug* (International Committee for Gliding Flight)		**TG**	Towed and released as glider (Appendix 4)
JFS	*Jagdfliegerschule* (Fighter pilots' school)		**TH**	*Technische Hochschule* (Technical university permitted to award degrees but not doctorates)
JG	*Jagdgeschwader* (Fighter wing)		**TR**	Towed and released, flight continued with rocket propulsion (Appendix 4)
KdE	*Kommando der Erprobungsstellen* (Headquarters, Test Centres)		**USAAF**	United States Army Air Force

ACKNOWLEDGEMENTS

We wish to extend our sincere thanks to all who served with EKdo 16, JG 400 and EJG 2 for the many forms of help we received and the hospitality we have been accorded by the *Traditionsgemeinschaft des JG 400* at their annual meetings. Also for the recollections and personal reports of the Allied pilots and aircrew, who faced the Me 163 in combat, and the US Army veterans who provided reminiscences and documents related to Brandis at the end of the war. We received generous help from Sven Carlsen, Uwe Frömert, Günther F Heise and Frank Schimpke (Brandis' historian), as well as Arthur Bentley, Eddie Creek and Robert Forsyth

during the preparation of this book. The authors also thank the staffs of the European Aeronautic & Defence Systems archives in Bremen and Ottobrunn, the Public Record Office, London, the National Archives, Maryland, the US Army Europe's Library and Resource Center, Heidelberg, and the DLR Archive, Göttingen, for their assistance in locating and providing access to source material.

And finally our thanks to Stephanie Ransom for translating the large number of original German documents, pilots' reminiscences and other information used as source material for this work.

INDEX